Critical incidents in teaching

Good teachers use good techniques and routines, but techniques and routines alone do not produce good teaching. The real art of teaching lies in teachers' professional judgement in circumstances where there is no 'right answer'. This combination of flexibility, informed guesswork and constant self-monitoring is not easy to acquire, but in this book David Tripp shows how teachers can draw on their own classroom expertise to develop it. He explains how to pinpoint 'critical incidents', those points at which a lesson either succeeds or fails, and how to analyse them in such a way as to draw out principles for future practice. Although the book raises important theoretic and methodological issues about teaching and research, it is primarily a practical guide grounded in numerous classroom examples and field-tested with teachers. Everyone concerned with the development of professionalism in teaching, and especially teachers who want to improve their own practice and to pass on their expertise to others will want to read it.

David Tripp has taught in a variety of schools in the UK and published widely in the fields of teacher education and professional development. He is now a Senior Lecturer in the School of Education, Murdoch University, Western Australia.

Critical incidents in teaching

Developing professional judgement

David Tripp

 RoutledgeFalmer
Taylor & Francis Group

LONDON AND NEW YORK

First published 1993
by Routledge
2 Park Square, Milton Park, Abingdon, Oxon OX14 4RN

Simultaneously published in the USA and Canada
by Routledge
270 Madison Ave, New York, NY 10016

Reprinted 1995, 2001 (twice), 2002 by RoutledgeFalmer

Transferred to Digital Printing 2003

RoutledgeFalmer is an imprint of the Taylor & Francis Group

© 1993 David Tripp

Typeset in Times by
Michael Mepham, Frome, Somerset
Digitally printed in Great Britain by
Butler and Tanner Ltd

British Library Cataloguing in Publication Data
A catalogue record for this book is available from the British Library

Library of Congress Cataloguing in Publication Data
A catalog record for this book is available from the Library of Congress

ISBN 0-415-09542-5 (hbk)
ISBN 0-415-09543-3 (pbk)

To my parents, Geo and Anne Tripp:
in belated recognition of some of the them in me.

... when horizons grow or diminish within a person the distances are not measurable by other people. Understanding grows from personal experience that enables a person to see and feel in ways so varied and so full of changeable meanings that one's self-awareness is the determining factor. Here one can admit more readily that the substances of a shadowy world are projected out of our personal thoughts, attitudes, emotions, needs. Perhaps it is easier to understand that even though we do not have the wisdom to enumerate the reasons for the behaviour of another person, we can grant that every individual does have his private world of meaning, conceived out of the integrity and dignity of his personality.

Virginia Axline: *Dibs: In Search of Self*

Contents

Figures

Index of critical incidents

Afterthought

The journey that led to this book began in 1978 when I found myself teaching a university course for in-service teachers entitled 'Classroom Research'. When I took it over, the course method was to expose teachers to summaries of the findings of the process–product classroom research industry, assisting them to identify areas and topics of interest related to their[1] own teaching situation, and supervising their design of a research project which they could perform to investigate an issue or problem. It was a common format, and seemed to work quite well in purely academic terms, although I was critical of the wholly quantitative methodology. In practical terms, however, the kinds of projects proposed were not only minute and trivial, but tended also to address questions that would generate academic rather than practical knowledge, thus connecting with and serving the interests of researchers rather than teachers.

Over the next year I realised that this was the result both of the kind of large-scale quantitative research promulgated by the literature in general and of the teacher's perception of the kind of issue that could be addressed by educational research. Drawing on my doctoral work in which I had been much influenced by the late Lawrence Stenhouse and his colleagues at the Centre for Applied Research in Education at Norwich, England, I helped the teachers design a more qualitative classroom action research project along the lines of those in *The Ford Teaching Project* (Elliott and Adleman 1976).

As a stimulus to discover issues to research, I presented students with separate research papers of the kind published in the *Review of Educational Research*. These covered ten issues, such as self-fulfilling prophecy, group work, questioning strategies and sexism, all of which were of major significance in terms of the amount and quality of the literature being published. The kind of topics chosen by the teachers were then much more appropriate, useful and interesting to them, but the course still failed in the important matter of the teachers relating the existing research to their own teaching: the topics which they chose were seldom the ones I had presented to them through the research reports.

At the time this bothered me because I believed that in a course about classroom research, teachers should concern and acquaint themselves with the major issues represented in the literature. Naïvely I believed that educational researchers would only invest such huge amounts of time, money, and energy in issues that were of importance to practising teachers. Among many others (Tom 1984; Popkewitz 1984), I later came to see how wrong those assumptions were (Tripp 1990a). Nevertheless, I attempted to demonstrate the relevance of the research to the teachers by asking them to look in their own classrooms for instances of the phenomena reported in the research. Topic after topic however, was greeted with objections such as, 'That's not what happens in my classroom', 'That's all very well in theory, but...', and 'It's too simplistic ... you can't just take that in isolation'. It was as if there were some kind of a plot to discount and belittle the expensive and magisterial pronouncements of the educational researchers.

Very well, I thought, on the mistaken assumption that the problem was essentially a lack of understanding and interest, Mohammed must come to the mountain. To encourage the teachers to take the research findings seriously with respect to their own teaching, I then began the course by asking the students to carry out classroom observations and interviews, recording them in journals which later became the critical incident research files of this book. The plan was that as they produced accounts of both the exceptional incidents occurring in their classrooms and the routine phenomena of their teaching, I would direct them to the research findings which they could then apply to their practice through action research.

However, what actually happened was that week after week the vast majority of journal items related only very distantly if at all to the existing research. They were concerned with matters such as whether students copying from each other was good or not, if it mattered that friendships changed so often, why students told so many tales on each other, the extent to which what happened before school affected formal learning, why students so often seemed to ignore instructions, and why teachers seemed to have to repeat things so often. I frequently waited in vain for the teachers to raise some of the major research issues that were my expertise and were dealt with in the literature. And when an issue such as 'labelling' did come up, they seemed to delight in producing examples from their own experience which provided data counter to the main effects reported.

With hindsight I could recognize two trends: first, that in contrast to the published research in which teacher and student behaviours and the overt and formal curriculum predominated, the teachers were raising practical matters instead; they were most often concerned with classroom management, and events closely but not obviously related to the hidden curriculum. Second, it seemed to require someone who was something of an outsider, a good analyst and already familiar with the research literature, to make the connections between a teacher's practice, the accounts of their practice as recorded in their critical incident files, and the literature on teaching.

At the time, I was just becoming aware of an uncomfortable contradiction in my position: I began to wonder why it was that I, like the teachers I was now teaching, had been considered very successful in the classroom when I, again like them, was totally ignorant of what I now was promulgating as knowledge essential to successful teaching. The answer dawned late but suddenly as I was lecturing to a curriculum class about the sociology of school knowledge. To illustrate the conflicts between the knowledge that school students valued and what they were actually taught, I read the following letter to a newspaper from a teacher about a typically 'schoolish' quiz it had published:

> I've been a teacher for 20 years and I answered the questions in your quiz as fast as I read them.
> But I don't know how a carburettor works; why Brunel's bridge doesn't fall down; what happens when you pass an electric current through water with salt or sugar in it; why it is dangerous to put gelignite in a bottle; the chemical composition of nylon; how you tell the time at the South Pole; the relative turning speed of a Spitfire and a Messerschmitt; or how the Holy Trinity 'works'. I have been asked all these (and more) by five-to-ten year olds, but never the questions in your quiz.
>
> (Open University 1973: 87)

While reading this aloud to the students, I suddenly realized that I was in exactly the same position as the teacher whose letter I was reading: as an educational researcher I was pursuing similarly institutionalized and partial knowledge about teaching which was just as irrelevant to the teachers whom I was teaching as was the author of the letter's to his students. The irony was that I was doing so at the very same time that I was teaching how various social processes and institutions have legitimated teachers' vested interests in the knowledge of school subjects at the expense of the students' interests. I saw for the first time that since I had left school teaching to become a university academic, my interests were now vested in answering questions which were primarily if not solely of interest to educational researchers, questions which were generally quite as unrelated to those of my in-service teachers as were those of that teacher to his students.

I can now identify the incident of the quiz as the probable starting point of this book because it was in dealing with it that I realized that I learned to improve and change my practice, not through the adoption of particular findings of 'educational' research, but through a close, personal, informed and critical examination of particular instances of my own practice. In fact, because the practical implications were my uppermost concern, I embarked upon a rather intuitive trial and error programme of action research which has led to the kind of work advocated here. It was the incident of the quiz which made me decide to try to learn how to work with teachers' experiences in a practical and scholarly fashion through the documentation and analysis of critical incidents in their practice, and which eventually led to the completion of this book.

When I came to look back at what I had written after finishing the first draft, however, I could see two major problems. First, it was altogether too idealistic. In view of the way teachers are educated and treated in our society, how could one expect them to strive for such a high standard of professionalism as was implied by my ideas? Second, I became more aware of some of the book's limitations and weaknesses, and wondered just how much it could therefore contribute towardss the realization of its ideals.

Then I was reminded of a paper written twenty years ago now by Flynn (1972), in which he raised the all-important question as to when a social project, innovation or idea should be evaluated. All too often the fate of an idea is determined by the success of the project in which it first happens to be tried. How often has a proposal been met with the comment 'That's already been tried in Europe (or America) by Smith (or Jones) and it doesn't work'. A particular project in a particular place at a particular time and run by particular people is taken as proof that there is no situation in which any version of the idea could ever work. In effect, just one of all the possible variants of an idea is tried once, one of the many ways of implementing it is used once; one particular method of one of the competing paradigms of research is used to evaluate it once... and a complex socially situated and constructed range of possibilities is rejected for evermore as if the trial were some simple and carefully controlled chemical reaction.

To illustrate the point, Flynn took the problem of knowing when would have been the right time and what would have been the right method to evaluate the idea that aircraft should replace rail and ship for safe, cheap, fast, long-distance passenger travel. Suppose the idea had been subjected to evaluation on the basis of the Wrights' first flight, which was, after all, thought to be the first true travel in a heavier-than-air machine. On the basis of their success, no responsible evaluator could have recommended further funding for the idea, even to the Pentagon. Or suppose one were to have evaluated their idea at the time of the first world war, by which time the plane had developed beyond recognition, yet it was still really only capable of short reconnaissance work on clear days. Even if one had evaluated the possibility of aircraft replacing rail and ship for long-distance passenger travel (or battleships for naval warfare) just before the Second World War, one could not have recommended continuation with the project.

Yet flying developed because it was not a single endeavour which could be submitted to a single evaluation. It grew because many different people made it happen. They liked flying, and they believed in the idea of its becoming commercially profitable. It was never allowed to be tied to a particular design. Each attempt was used for learning so that the next project began from an improved position.

I believe that I and many others share some revolutionary ideas about education that will be just as slow to realise as the development of the modern aircraft. One of these is that school teaching will one day be a profession in which the standards of practice will be as high as those in law and medicine because teachers, assisted by educational researchers, will understand their practice so well that every child will receive an education every aspect of which meets their own particular needs.

And, like the evolution of the modern aircraft, many separate ideas have to be put into practice and many different components to be invented, developed and tested before any overall progress is made. So this book demonstrates one aspect of teaching that represents but a small step towards the achievement of a professional ideal. People could evaluate this book in terms of that ideal. But no one can yet evaluate the ideal itself – if what humankind achieves in the physical world depends so much on what people wish for and strive to achieve, then how much more is the socially constructed world of teaching amenable to their turning a vision into reality?

I therefore hope that readers will use this book to imagine many new possibilities for education, and to consider in detail how one, the interpretation of critical incidents to inform professional judgement, could become a standard professional teaching practice. (I can be contacted by E-Mail as: tripp@murdoch.edu.au.)

David Tripp
Bedfordale
Western Australia
1993

Introduction: Teaching and research

TEACHERS, RESEARCHERS AND THE MEDIA

In some ways this is a book about educational research. Teachers have very good reasons to mistrust such books and regard them with apprehension. Teachers' fears are not unfounded; so often educational research, by investigating and thereby exposing the problems of schools, has been instrumental in giving them the bad press that they so often receive these days. And all too often researchers have used their perceptions of teachers' inadequacies to gain grants, publicity and to further their careers. Take for example, the main argument that the editor of a new journal was quoted as giving as the reason for yet another new publication:

> There has been a revolution in our knowledge about language in the past twenty years, and it's highly probable that lots of the practices that are being followed in schools in relation to developing children's language are quite wrong, misguided, even dangerous in their implications for the education of our kids.

So teachers are twenty years out of date and likely to be damaging children. Unsurprisingly, such attitudes make relationships between teachers and educational researchers very strained.[1] But even when a researcher goes out of their way to emphasise the achievements of an innovation, the press distort it to reflect poorly upon teachers.

For instance, in 1987 Colin Marsh, a colleague, evaluated initial progress on a new curriculum structure in a Western Australia school. His conclusion was that '... the introduction of the unit curriculum was a success... There were far more plusses than negatives...' and that overall, 'In a short period of time a number of notable successes have occurred... the few problems that were cited are not insurmountable.' However, under the headline, 'Schools' curriculum under fire', the state's only daily newspaper reported that 'big problems' had been found, which provoked further adverse comment from others in the media and community who had read only the newspaper report. The executive director of schools tried to set the record straight, but his response was made to appear subjective and partial by being published as a letter under the title, 'Support for the school curriculum', thereby suggesting merely that the director supported the new curriculum (in spite of the problems), but not that misreporting had occurred. The newspaper not only never admitted its inaccurate reporting, but also refused to publish a piece by the evaluator in which he explained the report and his findings.

Such incidents indicate that the press are a real problem. This perception is reinforced by events such as the following in which three university students were caught withdrawing cash from other people's accounts on false credit cards manufactured by the budding criminals themselves. When the case came to court, the lawyer for the defence stated that,

> Perhaps it is an indictment of our modern education system that it appears to have taught these three young men everything that is modern in technology but has failed to teach them anything correct in morality.
>
> (*The Western Mail* 15 Aug 1987: 18)

Such statements portray in a few lines a common public view: teachers are to blame for the personal and social problems of students. This statement does this in four major ways. First, it was the only part of the defence argument to be selected for central placing on the newspage in large, bold print, which suggests that it was the main, if not the only, cause of the problem. Nothing was said about any parental responsibility for moral matters, the bank's responsibility for their security systems, or the students' own responsibility for their deliberate criminal acts. Second, the article made only indirect reference to the fact that the youths actually got the idea from the media where the process they used was explained in all the necessary detail in a television programme. Third, the lawyer's comment was clearly approved of by the editorial staff, who obviously expected their readers to feel likewise. It also diverted readers' attention away from the media's part in the affair. Fourth, the comment managed to blame the education system for giving the students such highly sophisticated skills. One might be forgiven for imagining that giving students such skills was precisely what the education system should be doing, but the newspaper had managed to twist it so that a success of the education system actually discredited it.

So we are left with the obvious overall message that the thefts were not the fault of the young men themselves, their parents, the bank or the media, but solely the fault of the education system.

As a final irony, the article appeared in a paper that has consistently demanded the return of schools to a curriculum which concentrates more on basic technical skills and less on the humanities and social sciences; yet it is in these other subjects that one might expect moral education to occur. It was a contradiction of which neither the paper nor its readers seemed aware.

Such attitudes pervade the news media, so I have found it very difficult in my work to deal openly with the kind of problems that are an integral part of all professional practice. As an educator I have a duty to improve teachers' practice, a process that requires critique; as a member of the profession I also have a different duty to support those whose work I critique. I believe the way to achieve both is always to place a problem in the broader context of teachers' professional practice. As in all professions, practitioners will always make mistakes occasionally; but too often people blame a teacher for what they see as an error of judgement because they do not know or understand the conditions under which the teachers have to make their professional judgements. Research that ignores the way in which the conditions of teachers' work affect their practices presents a highly simplified and very negatively biased picture of them and their work. So, although there are a number of incidents in this book in which teachers are shown to be less than perfect, I have always tried to show how more often than not it is a matter of their best intentions being thwarted or transformed by factors beyond their control. I have also tried to show how, in contrast to most media and many research reports, the professional norm is that teachers make excellent judgements in extremely complex and difficult circumstances. Typical evidence of this is given in the next section.

TEACHER EXPERTISE

Incident 1: Settling down 1

The first lesson of my first teaching experience. I pause outside the door to steel myself for the row going on inside. I walk in. A few heads turn, but if anything the noise increases. *Be confident: act as if you know you'll get what you want.* 'Alright then.' I say loudly. More heads turn. 'Hey, you lot, I said "be quiet".'

'No you didn't, you said it was alright.' An unidentifiable voice from the back. Tittering.

Well that's quietened them, anyhow. 'I meant you to be quiet', I say, seeking to identify the nuisance; but there are too many students still standing up for me to see every one.

'Why didn't you say so then?'

A voice from someplace I'm not looking at. Again I fail to identify it. I hesitate and stupidly notice I'm sweating. *This can't go on. The best defence is attack.* 'Who said that?' Total silence for the first time. All eyes brighten, as if something interesting's about to happen. *But who was it? Each of the many faces looks equally innocent and very unhelpful.* 'I want to know who spoke just then.'

'You did.' Laughter. Nasty raucous got-you-so-there type laughter. Aha, I saw that, a large fair-haired boy slouching against the back wall.

'Very clever. Remarkably clever for someone who finds the normal conventions of the English language so impenetrable.' *Sarcasm. You were never going to use sarcasm as a weapon when you became a teacher. You've opened your mouth just four times so far, and you're right into it. Try to find some common ground.* 'Look, whether you like it or not, we've no choice: we're going to be together five hours a week, so we might as well learn to get along. I can't carry on a conversation if I don't know who's talking to me. Besides which it's bad manners.'

'Big deal.' Tittering

Damn. Missed it again. Someone over there, a girl, I think. 'For you, maybe.' *More sarcasm, that brings it to 33 per cent of what I've said so far. Quick, something else. Try another tack.* 'OK, so I said "alright" but meant "shut up"; do you think you should always say exactly and literally what you mean?'

'Yes, if you know what "literally" means, that is.' More laughter.

Yes, same voice, that girl there. Looks pretty sharp. Never mind, we're talking. 'OK, suppose I said to you,... um ... um.'

'I wouldn't know what you were talking about.'

More laughter. Even louder, but genuine amusement this time. I laugh too, and get real grins back. *That's it: show them you're human.*

'Hey, give us a break. No, I'm trying to think of something we say but we don't really mean.' *Why can't I think of a single metaphor? I'm going to 'do metaphors' with them next week. No, wait a moment, a greeting.* 'OK, if I said to you, "Good day", what would I mean?'

'Have a good day.'

'It's a good day.'

'Hello.'

Great! Three sensible responses. Now we're getting somewhere. But they're meant to respond one at a time. 'OK don't just shout out.' *That's pretty negative: respond to what they say, don't just judge how they say it.* 'But I've not actually said any of those things, have I? And anyway, which do I really mean; or doesn't it matter?' *Too many questions. Remember to ask only one question at a time. But they've all sat down now, and they're listening. It'll be OK I know I can handle this lot.*

Incident 2: Settling down 2

A teacher enters a very noisy classroom to start the lesson.
    Teacher: Rick, is that you making all the noise?
    Rick: No Sir!
    Teacher: Well then, who is making all the noise?
The class noise subsides as students take interest in the conversation between the teacher and Rick. Silence. The teacher looks round all areas of the classroom.

As with any skill, something a beginner finds very difficult is effortless to the real expert. In contrast to what I, as a beginning teacher, eventually achieved accidentally in Incident 1, the very experienced teacher in Incident 2 walked into the classroom and immediately singled out an individual. Experienced teachers have a large repertoire of such techniques for subduing noisy classes. This one works by turning attention towards a particular and therefore limited interaction of which the teacher is in control. And, though it's only actually transacted between the teacher and a single student, the event becomes a focus for the whole class whose attention remains on the teacher when the exchange is terminated. The teacher controls the event, and thereby controls the class.

But does employing the technique as expertly as the second teacher did, mean that he or she is a professional, or rather merely a thoroughly competent practitioner? Being able to do something and knowing how one does it are two different aspects of being professional about something. Understanding what it is one does and how one does it, however, involves a different aspect of professionalism: it is a matter of being intellectually expert about expert practice. It is in learning from experience that these two come together: one does, and one thinks about how and what one is doing. So although most people become expert practitioners through actually doing the job, skilled professional teaching is also an intellectual matter.

For most teachers the intellectual side of their expert performance consists of two kinds of reflection: evaluation ('Did it work? What else could/should I have done? How could I do it better?'), and common wisdom (there is more to discipline than merely maintaining it: how the students feel about being disciplined affects how they will respond next time). These ideas are a kind of craft knowledge, some of which is included in teachers' pre-service education, but is more often transmitted by experts to novices as on-the-job advice. Lots of this craft knowledge was running through my mind in Incident 1: be confident; act as if you know you will get what you want; identify a nuisance quickly; respond to what they say; only listen to those you choose to answer; and so on. So a teacher who was acting reflectively would not only observe whether silence was achieved or not, but would also consider the way in which the student's feelings had been handled and whether to accept an uninvited answer because it was a useful one. Not all teachers are that reflective, of course, though more are becoming so as our knowledge of what good teachers do increases, and as more teachers are taught how to reflect upon their practice. At present, however, it is principally skillful action learned through experience that constitutes the professional expertise of most teachers.

Reflective teaching is therefore essential to a professional approach to practice. But in all the major professions there is another intellectual ingredient of practice: being able to explain and thereby justify what one does through a more knowledgeable, rigorous, and academic analysis. This does not appear to be necessary in teaching because few teachers are taught, and so far as I know none are required, to do it. The second lesson extract was part of a lesson transcript made for part of an assignment in a higher degree course in education. A teacher brought it to me saying he had recorded a lesson, but could not think of anything to say about it as nothing 'in particular' had happened. This suggests that although the teacher is professional in what he does (he is so expert a practitioner, in fact, that he takes his skill totally for granted), but he is not professional in the sense of possessing an understanding of how he has done it, nor does he possess the means of gaining that understanding. One kind of expertise is required to make a lesson happen, and a very different kind of expertise and knowledge to diagnose what actually went on in it. Many teachers have learned to use the 'single interaction' technique of subduing a whole class, but few could provide more than the basic explanation of how it worked than I have already given. Academic skills, however, are very powerful tools which, when applied to apparently simple practices, yield some interesting insights. So let us have another look at the analysis of Incident 2 in a slightly more academic fashion to see what really happened.

A common form of analysis is to examine the language used, but few teachers are taught to do this in their professional education. Here the teacher began by saying, 'Rick, is that you making all the noise?' One notices that this teacher knows who to pick on and what his name is, important information not available to me in Incident 1. But more interesting is the fact that the teacher seems to have said something rather silly: he was asking a single boy if he was solely responsible for what was obviously a whole class noise. Why should the teacher do that? By asserting something that was patently untrue, the teacher was actually providing a let-out for the student: it was a nonsensical accusation which the student could sensibly and legitimately deny, even if he were a prominent noise maker, because a single student could only contribute to whole class noise, not make it alone. Thus the teacher, while calling attention to the noise Rick was making, actually made Rick appear more rational and sensible than the teacher who was disciplining him. The accusation had the same effect as if it had been true, but because it quite clearly was not, the teacher did not then have to admonish or punish the student. The teacher then deliberately continued to assert that there must be one person making all the noise ('Well then, who is making all the noise?') which, with his gaze directed at everyone in the room, told the others that he was about to pick on someone else, so they all stopped talking. Without anyone being punished or losing face, the whole class was instantly and effectively silenced, and apparently simply because the teacher structured a false accusation around the word 'all'. If the approach were informed by craft knowledge it would probably be something like, 'Pick on individuals'; and, at a more reflective level, 'The key to good discipline is to maintain it without building resentment and thereby producing further resistance'. One can only admire the technical expertise of teachers who develop such ways of achieving it.

Such skill is of a level and kind that is much more akin to practice in the major professions such as medicine and law, than it is like that of craftspeople such as carpenters or motor mechanics. It is also important to recognise that all competent teachers possess such skills and experience to perform in classrooms in that way. So why is it that teachers do not have the social status, conditions of work and material rewards of medics and barristers? One reason is that so few people, even those within the profession (teachers included), are aware of what teachers actually do, or of their impact on their clients. Teachers, like the one in the example above, who display all the qualities of skill and experience as they go about the routine of their job, who reflect on their practice in such a way that it continues to remain successful over the years, are in one sense highly professional. But if they are not also able to articulate the specialist conduct knowledge or the judgements that underlie what they do, they are in another sense craftspeople rather than professionals.

This book suggests a way to deal with that issue. I argue that more than general or evaluative reflection upon merely technical expertise acquired through experience is necessary for teachers to be professional in a way that would enable them to overcome their poor public image and achieve the status of a profession for their work. I suggest that teachers should be diagnostic in the sense that they are able to employ profession-specific knowledge and expertise to recognise, describe, understand and explain their practice in an academic fashion, and to interpret that diagnosis in order to form expert professional judgements to further the well-being of their clients. The method advocated here for achieving this form of practice involves the identification and analysis of incidents such as those already described. Overall, the aim of this book is to offer a practical approach to teaching and classroom research that opens a way to improve practice in the profession of education as a whole.

THE ROLE OF THIS BOOK

While it is generally recognised that teaching is currently in a crisis, the underlying ways in which teacher education and the educational research industry have contributed to that crisis are less obvious but more in need of reform. This book suggests some immediate practical action and longer-term aims that may be instrumental in helping to overcome that crisis.

More than anything else, it is a book about the nature, achievement and value of what is generally called 'professional judgement': those expert guesses which result from combining experience with specialist theoretical knowledge. It is argued that teachers' work lacks public status because they are seen more to draw on the recall of 'right answers' rather than having to use their judgement.

That is not a new problem, for it has already been addressed by at least three research and teacher development traditions, each of which has had but limited success. In the process-product classroom research approach, summarised by people such as Dunkin and Biddle (1974), teachers tend to be excluded from the research agenda and processes (which are often irrelevant or damaging to teachers) and they do not use the findings in their practice. In the action research and Stenhouse's teacher-as-researcher approaches (Elliott and Adleman 1976; Stenhouse 1975) teachers work as researchers under such powerful constraints that, despite considerable and sustained efforts in a number of countries, they have actually contributed very little through their research to specialist academic educational knowledge as a whole, achieving instead some personal and private professional development. And in the reflective practitioner tradition (now associated with Schön 1983), teachers tend to draw on personal and general rather than specialist theoretical knowledge as the basis for their judgements.

This book suggests that the development of professional judgement through the diagnosis and interpretation of critical incidents is another alternative which will lead to what might be called 'diagnostic teaching'. A diagnostic teacher is one who can analyse their practice in a scholarly and academic fashion to produce expert interpretations upon which to base and justify their professional judgements.

That ideal and the method of achieving it outlined in this book are, I believe, particularly valuable in regard to two important and rapidly developing trends: the attempt to specify good teaching in terms of a set of observable competencies, and the move towards the removal of teacher education from universities to re-site it in schools. Unless this is to produce a form of straight apprenticeship training, teacher-educators have to find new ways to teach in school situations the professional academic knowledge that has hitherto been taught on campuses. Working in an academic fashion with novice and experienced teachers to understand their everyday working experience is clearly one way to turn to advantage the increased time spent in schools.

CRITICAL INCIDENTS

People often ask what a critical incident is and how to recognise one. The answer is, of course, that critical incidents are not 'things' which exist independently of an observer and are awaiting discovery like gold nuggets or desert islands, but like all data, critical incidents are created. Incidents happen, but critical incidents are produced by the way we look at a situation: a critical incident is an interpretation of the significance of an event. To take something as a critical incident is a value judgement we make, and the basis of that judgement is the significance we attach to the meaning of the incident. This is dealt with in detail in Chapter 2; for now, let us analyse another example to show what makes it critical.

In principle, we can read any and everything that happens in a critical fashion. Often the events we notice and remember are just routine things we feel good or unhappy about, or things that amuse us, like this one.

Incident 3: The horse butterfly

The teacher had just completed a fairly clear lesson on insects, their characteristics, etc. She then chose individual children to move about like an insect of their choice, and about six of the children hopped and wriggled around. One of the children who had not been chosen to perform, frantically waved his hand to attract the teacher's attention, but the teacher did not choose him. She then went to her desk and picked up a painted butterfly and started to explain how she wanted the children to make one like it. The boy said in a loud voice, 'Oh Miss, I wish you'd've chosen me, I'd've been a horse.' 'No you couldn't,' another boy said, 'that's not an insect.' The teacher heard only the last part and said, 'Of course it is, it's a butterfly,' and went on with her instructions. The second boy said nothing at all, but sat looking at the first boy in great puzzlement.

At one level this incident is, of course, just amusing. But judging from some of the things the teachers of my own children have been credited with, this kind of misunderstanding is a very common occurrence in classroom communication. It is a special kind of misunderstanding, however, because the student did not misunderstand the teacher's actual words, nor the teacher the boy's; the misunderstanding occurred because they each included the other's words into their own quite separate context. Further, it was a failure of communication rather than understanding, but the result was that the student was left with misinformation. By definition then, misunderstandings of this type cannot be picked up by the students or the teacher, because when they are detected they are corrected immediately, and cease to be a misunderstanding. On this occasion we were able to see the genesis of the misunderstanding only because there was an observer present.

Deciding what kind of an event it was is the first step towards understanding it; but to turn the event into a critical incident something more than merely categorising it has to be done. We have to ask both what happened and what allowed or caused it to happen, which means we have to describe some of the deeper structures that produce that kind of incident. One of those structures is the hidden curriculum, a part of which is the mythology (in Barthes' [1973] sense of the word) of schooling. It is not difficult to suggest two myths that appear to be operating here: the teacher knows everything, and the teacher is always right. Another part of the hidden curriculum is the unstated procedural rules of classroom learning. Here, the rule the boy seems bound by is not to argue with the teacher unless invited to do so. The result was that although the teacher's assertion clearly conflicted deeply with the boy's existing knowledge and understanding, he overtly and at least temporarily accepted the misinformation. The incident may now be said to be critical in that it shows several different aspects of the hidden curriculum, namely, the asymmetry of the classroom speech situation and students' valuation of their understanding in relation to that of their teacher.

Interestingly, for it only happens rarely, this incident may also be critical in terms of the child's social and intellectual development. Believing what is patent nonsense from a teacher may be the norm at this age, but children (to a greater or lesser extent) do grow out of the habit as they become more confident of their own knowledge and understanding. It may be that such a serious conflict in knowledge between a student and a teacher serve to sow the first seeds of doubt in a young student's mind, and will enable them later to challenge their teachers rather than just to accept everything they say. So this incident is also an example of a critical incident in the original historical sense of the term, because it could mark an important change or turning point in this learner's biography.

A final point about this incident is that we obviously need to discover more precisely the nature and extent of such taken for granted attitudes, how they are reproduced in succeeding generations of students, how they are maintained in what kinds of classrooms, and how they are resisted and overcome by which children as they develop. So this incident also raises yet another important teaching issue about which there is very little educational research.[2]

ORGANISATION OF THE BOOK

Although this book is in many ways a fairly straightforward 'how to do it' account of critical incidents, the main agenda has to do with the idea that it is professional judgement which makes teaching a profession rather than a technically expert occupation or vocation. I therefore begin with the idea that the kind of technical routines that are essential to all teaching cannot be simply set and followed, but need constant monitoring and change, a process in which critical incidents are essential.

The first chapter outlines the importance of achieving a shift from an unquestioning technical approach in which one simply asks, 'How am I going to do this?' to an approach which involves asking questions such as, 'How am I going to decide what ought I to do, and how can I justify why I ought to do it?'

The main part of the book which then follows is about the nature, creation and use of critical incidents. I deal in some detail with a number of ways of analysing critical incidents, the construction of a critical incident file and two specific uses of critical incidents, in autobiography and for social critique. The final chapter returns to a reconsideration of the professional nature of teaching, and the conclusion looks at critical incidents in relation to the study of teaching.

ACKNOWLEDGEMENTS

First I wish to thank all the six hundred West Australian teachers with whom I have been privileged to work over the past decade. They not only contributed many of the incidents which are incorporated into the book, but also helped me to develop and trial the whole critical incident method. I am enormously indebted and grateful to them all for their incidents, and, with apologies to any whom I may have missed, I would like to thank the following by name: Karen Baker, John Beattie, Gerardina Benato, Rosemary Brown, Inez-Maree Bulbrook, Maureen Chandler, John Colgan, Oliver Cosgrove, Patricia Dougal, Peter Fowlie, Paul Ganderton, Michael Greenacre, Marilyn Hand, Margaret Herley, Sylvie Herron, Jim Heslop, Margaret Hodgkin, Angela Innes-Brown, Pamela Judge, Marian Kemp, Rosemary Kinsey, Cecila Kinsella, Cherylyn Legerstee, Delphine McFarlane, Susan Mcgirr, Wayne Martino, Janet Moore, Tony Mordini, Kerris Myers, Anne Napolitano, David Nockolds, Tim O'Keefe, Jeanette Paulik, Dick Pot, Glenys Richards, Fiona Ross, Jean Rowland, Bethwyn Saunders, Gail Smart, John Thomson, Dianne Tomazos, Maria Vajda and John Woodley.

I am also greatly indebted to Marguerite Laurence, my resident editor, who has not just encouraged and supported me through the many drafts over the past two years, but has read and re-read them, clarifying my thinking and improving the overall readability enormously. Thanks, Marguerite, and thanks too to my father, Geo Tripp, for his thorough reading of the first draft.

Finally, thanks to Stella Eversden for her proofing, referencing and producing the initial index, and to other colleagues for their encouragement, ideas and feedback. In particular I would like to mention John Ackland, Andy Hargreaves, Peter Grimmett, Bob Hodge, Antoinette Oberg, Annette Patterson, John Smith, Rob Walker, and John Watt.

Chapter 1

Problematic and practice

Incident 4: Music prize

*My 11-year-old daughter came back from school and told me with great
excitement that she had won a prize in music.*

That's really good. A prize?... How many prizes were there?

Just two.

And which was yours, first or second?

I got the girls' prize.

And there was a boys' prize?

Yes.

Was that fair, one for each?

Oh yes. There's always one for the girls and one for the boys.

But supposing you were second best girl so you didn't get the girls' prize,
would it be fair that a boy who was not so good as you got one just because he
was a boy?

Of course it would, otherwise the boys would never get one.

INTRODUCTION

Reflecting on what we do is essential to the development of professional judgement, but unless our reflection involves some form of challenge to and critique of
ourselves and our professional values, we tend to simply reinforce existing patterns
and tendencies. The problem is that reflection does not take place in a social and
psychological vacuum; so-called 'objectivity' is always partial because perception
and thought are always contextualised and therefore limited. Reflection is always
informed by a view of the world which is created by our culture, values and
experiences. This forms a circularity that reinforces our existing view of the world:
we construct our world through reflection, but how and on what we reflect is largely
determined by our existing world view. It is this tendency which means that we
have to do something other than merely reflect upon our practice to change it or
view it differently. We first must change our awareness through deliberately setting
out to view the world of our practice in new ways. In other words, to develop our

professional judgement, we have to move beyond our everyday 'working' way of looking at things, and this chapter is about how critical incidents can help us to do so.

In this chapter I want to look at our professional awareness in two different ways: one has to do with the things we do actually notice about our practice and which we are therefore aware of; the other is an underlying structure which both limits and facilitates what we consciously and unconsciously choose to attend to. To distinguish the two, I shall refer to the former as awareness, and the latter as problematic. Beginning with the first, there are, of course, degrees of awareness which, at their simplest, have been defined by Polanyi and Prosch (1975) as 'focused' and 'subsidiary'. This distinction is important because these notions incorporate recognition of the fact that we can be more or less aware of things. These terms also emphasise the active role of the individual in the process of being aware: being aware is something that we do actively for ourselves, rather than something that is done to us. Nevertheless, over time we do structure our awareness so that we do not always consciously control it. So while the structure of our existing awareness tends to determine for us what is to be focused upon and what is more and less important, we can also deliberately question and change such things. This control is empowering because it enables us to take responsibility for developing our own awareness.

Furthermore, the different kinds of awareness suggest a way of developing an agenda of aspects of our practice that we can critique: what pleases or bothers us are often things of which we have a background awareness, but have not properly focused on. An obvious example is our routines. Routines are always present, but for much of the time we have to employ them quite unthinkingly because it is not possible to subject every routine to constant rigorous examination. Yet, like any habit, routines are not always quite what they seem and their effects are not always the same, nor are they without side-effects. So it is important to regularly focus our awareness on them.

That is not to say that we should, or indeed could, always have our attention focused on our routines, or we would be like some classroom Hamlet, inhibiting action with a numbing thoughtfulness. So, while the strength of routines is that they enable us to do things without consciously attending to them, that is also their danger. So we also need to focus on our routines periodically.

In general then, it is possible, and I believe essential to a professional performance, always to be consciously focusing our awareness on some aspect of practice, and so to become aware of as many aspects as possible over time. What is being closely observed and questioned is thus our focused awareness. What has been or will at some other time be focused upon, is our subsidiary awareness, the main point of the distinction being that we can change the focus of our awareness.

Problematic

The idea of 'problematic' is important to professional consciousness because it provides the best connection to other work existing in the related field of a critical approach to theory in the natural and social sciences. Problematic has to do with the kind of things which are seen to be problems and the kind of information sought to provide the kind of answers which are accepted as reasonable solutions to them. Unfortunately the term has become confused through having been used as a jargonistic adjective for something which is a problem: 'You know we were going to meet for lunch on Tuesday? Well, I'm afraid that's a bit problematic now.' Problematic the noun,[1] however, is much more than that: it is the theoretical structure which causes the phenomenon in question to be seen as a problem.[2]

The first time I consciously realised how problematic informs our action was observing the following incident (Tripp 1986: 37).

Incident 5: Doing too much

Chris came into the staffroom saying, 'Julie Jones says her Dad's going to come down here tomorrow and break both my arms and legs!'

Interested chorus of, 'Why, what've you done to her?'

'I told them to do nine of the twelve questions for homework and she did all twelve, so I took a mark off her score.'

In response to general censorship, he replied, 'Well, it'll teach her a lesson. When she does the exam she'll remember she has to do exactly what she's told. She won't forget that now.'

And of course, he was probably quite right that she would not forget; but for us the problem we immediately saw was that deducting marks for making an extra effort could so adversely affect Julie's attitude and future effort that she would not do well in the exam even if she did read the instructions correctly. It was not that Chris was any less concerned about Julie doing well in the course, but that he saw the major determinant of exam performance as being correct reading of the instructions. It was this divergence in view about learning that led to different aspects of the incident being seen as a problem.

It is our problematic which leads us to develop and uncritically rely upon a set of structured practices which are employed in more or less similar ways upon more or less similar occasions, and which are generally called routines (Berger and Luckmann 1971), and in this case, 'professional routines'. These professional routines are constructed by and enacted through a particular problematic, and are, by definition, seldom if ever challenged or consciously engaged. It is these routines which thus effectively determine what we actually do in the social and material world of our professional practice. Problematic is a useful concept because it is only when it is realised that problematics exist that one can set out to expose, understand and acknowledge (or, if necessary, transform) them.[3]

Consider the following that was a more recent example:

Incident 6: Group competition

Anne-Marie was concerned about the way that her 12-year-old students seemed unable to discuss things with each other, so she divided the class into groups, giving half the groups the task of developing an argument for something, the other half, against it. She then had them debate the issue, group against group. I asked if she thought that asking people to co-operate in developing a wholly one-sided position that they didn't necessarily agree with in order to use it to oppose the views of other people was a good idea. She said, no, it wasn't a good idea, it was an obvious problem, but that she'd never seen it like that.

In other words, there was a problem with what she was doing, but because co-operation–competition antithesis was not part of the categories in which she habitually thought, she had not seen the implicit contradiction and certainly not that the activity could be characterised as subliminal training in bigotry.

It is problematics which structure such absences and invisibilities in our professional awareness. They produce in us a disposition not to see that there is a regular pattern to the hiding of what is hidden. That might sound complicated, but its effects are often blindingly obvious. We can take for another example the day my eldest daughter came home from school with a prize for music (Incident 4) which I narrated at the start of this chapter. First, she knew two important facts about her world: one, that prizes were awarded for merit; second, that the criteria of merit were varied for different groups. The reason that she did not see any contradiction between these two facts was that her notion of 'fairness' included the idea of equal distribution between groups. But that is not a necessary or indeed the only way of being fair. On the one hand, in most realms of life prizes are not distributed evenly between groups; and on the other, even at school prizes (unlike paints and books) are seldom distributed evenly within groups, which is the more usual childhood notion of fairness. So it becomes apparent that the notion of fairness varies in ways that are commonly accepted by teachers and children alike according to what is being distributed.

There is, however, nothing necessarily fair about such variation: it is only fair in terms of particular values. In the case of this music prize the whole idea of fairness has been constructed with gender considerations so firmly embedded into it that the idea of awarding prizes on merit alone has come to be seen as unfair. Because the practice was a normal routine no one saw the underlying problematic, so they did not challenge it. Such structures are well hidden, but the messages they generate are very explicit: my daughter unerringly read that it is not fair for girls to compete on equal terms with boys if they can do something better than them.[4]

In practical terms, what comes out of all of this is that if we do not control our professional awareness and problematics, then they control us. The aspects of our professional awareness that are most amenable to critique are probably those which have come from academic theory, because all educational theories are partial and there are many alternative theories to choose from. Other aspects, such as our attitudes towards our students, because they are produced in a more diffuse culture than that of educational research, are less amenable to articulation and hence to informed challenge. A major problem is that they are subjectively held, a fact that is clearly and constantly revealed in our discussions with our colleagues.

The practical problematic

What seems to me to be perhaps the greatest disaster of modern education is an over-dichotomised theory/practice relation: it enables academics to pursue theory without regard to the practical realities of classrooms, and enables teachers to dismiss theory as irrelevant. Unfortunately, the latter view results in what could be called the 'practical problematic', which, because it ignores all but the one form of interpretation, is perhaps the most insidious occupational hazard of teaching. I write that because it is a problematic which regulates deliberate action only in terms of what to do and how, without critically informing that action. The practical problematic both ensures that perception is limited to procedural problems and it prevents strategic action because it means that the question we ask when faced with a problem is, 'What shall we do about it?' It thereby excludes such prior diagnostic questions as why it is that we want to do what we do and how we do it.

The fact that much of our deliberate action is composed of taken-for-granted routines means that our practical problematic has as its sphere of influence the generation and maintenance, adaptation and reform, of routines. In other words, it is the practical problematic which determines that when we do focus our awareness on our routines, we do so in order to make them work better rather than to challenge them on, for instance, grounds of social justice.

The practical problematic is powerful precisely because whether something works or not is the ultimate test of a strategy or routine. But in making something work our awareness is turned away from questioning the terms in which it is said to 'work'. A professional working within the practical problematic is one whose awareness is exclusively turned to setting out to find a way to get something done without considering, for instance, in whose interests it ought to be done, or even what has produced the circumstances in and about which action is required. For instance, teachers frequently set out to reduce the amount of noise during a particular activity, without any consideration of the significance of the noise itself, or the underlying social relations which generally make it a problem for the teacher alone. Such questions are largely irrelevant if the test of a good teacher is limited to whether they can keep the class quiet or not, and the routines by which they keep the class quiet need never be challenged on any other grounds. There are thus very good reasons for the practical problematic to be so ubiquitous and powerful.

The practical problematic is normal in teaching because it is the nature of classrooms that for much of the time the teacher faces many simultaneous and conflicting demands for immediate attention and action. That being the case, effective and efficient routines are inevitably necessary. But so much skill, time and energy are necessary merely to operate the routines that there is very little left for reflection. However, most teachers recognise that just because a routine works it is not necessarily a good routine: there are many other factors to be considered in determining its value. We all need to be able to justify our routines on other grounds, and it is here that theories come into play once again. To ensure we can publicly account for the value of our routines, we tend to selectively employ those aspects of those educational theories which lend support to what we find we have to do anyway. It is our professional awareness which gives rise to our set of pedagogic constructs concerning, for instance, the nature of classroom learning, motivation, discipline, achievement, individual differences and so on. At that level they are essentially theoretical constructs in the sense that they are to be found in the literature of researched knowledge about education; they will have been learned through academic discourses; and they will have been constructed in order to describe and explain teaching in general, not the teaching of a particular teacher or lesson.

Although the result of a practical problematic is action which is thus doubly determined by things other than a theorisation of our practice, the routines themselves are so very obvious that it is possible to use them to work on both our problematic and our awareness. In operating routines, we can expose our problematic by posing the kind of questions about our practice which we do not usually ask of ourselves. It is that analysis of our problematic which leads us to confront our professional values and judgements. The final result should be the kind of radical professional consciousness so much sought recently (Smyth 1985). The professional education of teachers has to take much more into account the way educational theories are individually perceived, mediated and reconstructed by practitioners.

The point of this is that it is most often the practical problematic which provides the entry point into an increased awareness of other features of our professional practice. It is very easy to show both a teacher who already has a quiet class and one who has a noisy class and wants to know how best to quieten it (the practical problematic), that they are operating certain routines with regard to noise, and hence must consider first what educational theories might be informing what they do. Second, to begin to work on the dispositions that have led them to adopt these theories and to seek less noise.

Most teachers realise that, although their routines may originally have been consciously planned and practised, they will have become habitual, and so unconscious, as expertise is gained over time. Indeed, our routines often become such well-established habits that we often cannot say why we did one thing rather than another, but tend to put it down to some kind of mystery such as 'professional intuition' or simply 'knowing'.

Many people, and teachers are no exception, are actually very interested in knowing more about how they operate, for that knowledge increases their power and effectiveness. Critical incidents can be very important in that process because they provide a means of enabling teachers to be more aware of the nature of their professional values and associated problematics, to question their own practice, and to concretise their generally abstract notions of values such as social justice.

All of these processes are deeply theoretical, the implications of which is beyond the scope of this exploration. Here I want to move on to the issue of how our problematic affects our practice.

PROBLEMATISING TEACHING THROUGH A CRITICAL INCIDENT FILE ENTRY

It is important to remember that teachers' critical incident file entries are by definition their experiences and ideas, and if they can be used to find a starting point for further or action research, then that authenticity tends to carry over. As a collaborative action research facilitator, I use the critical incident file to help teachers to identify, articulate and examine their professional awareness and problematic, not to direct what they should do. Direction, if any, comes in the form of asking difficult questions, of asking them to take account of how I see things. As one teacher said, 'You always seem to make trouble for me, but it's useful trouble.' Because almost all teachers come to their practice with a practical problematic, the trouble I make is to use their critical incidents to turn that problematic into a theoretical one. That is a simple, but often a very powerful, process; and it is one which is perhaps better illustrated then explained. So here is my account of the first occasion when I realised the potential of using critical incidents in that way.

Incident 7: Finishing work

John didn't finish his work again today. Must see he learns to complete what he has begun.

The entry revealed that the teacher's problematic was essentially practical, so no questions about why it should be done could arise. The teacher had noted a phenomenon (John was not finishing his work), which she had categorised as a problem, and wanted to move straight on to finding a solution to it. That is often the case when the only forms of interpretation employed are the practical and reflective, the teacher takes the problem as given and only reflects on how to solve it. Thus in this case, the problem was John's deviance, and the only solution was for him to conform, the means to which end were to be found in the teacher's craft knowledge. It was perceived simply as a matter of how to get John to learn to do something he should do.

Of course, it is possible to work on that problematic, but if the recorded phenomenon itself is questioned, then many other kinds of solution are possible. This is most obviously and easily done by changing the observation into a question, so that 'John didn't finish his work again today.' becomes, ' Why did John not finish his work today?' or the more general, 'Why is John not finishing his work?' Thus, the very fact that the initial observation is stated in terms of the practical problematic, provides a good entry for a facilitator to work on the teacher's habitual thinking. In this case, the teacher's statement that her problem was how to get John to finish his work, exposed her value that the students need or ought (to be made) to finish their work.

When I challenged this, at first the teacher defended her initial position, simply saying that children have to finish their work because it is necessary for learning, it is good for them, it is expected, if some did not then none would,... and so on. But she then quickly recognised that making all students always finish all their work did not necessarily follow, and was in fact an aspect of her 'professional habitus', that is an unconscious and unexamined value which had been taken for granted or 'lived', rather than having been questioned and rationally thought through. The point here is that the critical incident file entry made very obvious an aspect of practice that might benefit from critique.

Having seen that there might be an issue, the next stage was to explore it in terms that would shift the problematic from the practical towards the critical, that is to the educational reasons and personal values that might underlie the current practice and any subsequent strategic action. So the kind of questions I asked were:

1 Why did (does) John not finish his work?
2 Why should he finish it?
3 How does he see the tasks demanded of him?
4 Are the tasks the right kind, quality and quantity?

Such questions constitute the kind of 'reconnaissance' from which action research sequences are generally entered. To answer the first question, the teacher must systematically monitor, examine and explain John's behaviour, because one should not proceed on guesses about motives and causes, but ascertain them as accurately as the situation will allow. Clearly if John was not completing his work because he was lazy (the teacher's explanation at this point), then the appropriate action would be quite different from what it would be were he not completing his work for the reason that he was hungry, tired, bored or blind.

The second question had already been raised in a preliminary fashion, with a recognition that what she did was a matter of values. Any examination of values tends to lead either to an acknowledgment that how things are is necessarily and immutably how things must be (reification), or that this is how things should and ought to be (belief). These are important points to arrive at because they can be challenged and then worked through to develop an understanding of the way in which what at first appear to be unchangeable givens often turn out to be relatively local if not personal human choices. At a more complex macro level they can be seen as social structures of human manufacture, not natural laws of the material universe.

Underlying the third question was another issue: the fact that the teacher did not know what John thought about it all confronts the fact that there was an asymmetry of power between the teacher and the student that limited her (rather than his[5]) knowledge. That was a constraint the teacher placed upon the situation herself. There was very little John could do about it once the teacher's mind was made up and he was labelled 'lazy'. But it was something the teacher could act upon unilaterally. A first move towards making any power distribution more equitable is to discover the point of view of others, which in this case meant encouraging the student to express his view. Even though any single view must be regarded as a partial, limited and perhaps suspect view of the whole situation, it is obviously essential information.

The last was more obviously practical, though how it would be answered would depend entirely upon the answers to the previous three. One can see, then, that the case I am making is not against practical questions, but that they should come last rather than first. To set out to answer her original question the teacher not only needed to look at what she thought the situation was, but also to judge how sure she was about it and what was the best action to take. That judgement could be informed by educational theory as well as by her existing craft knowledge.

Just to complete the picture I am trying to build around this case, its actual history is relevant. The entry was made by a teacher a fortnight into the critical incident file writing phase of the action research course I was running. Up to that point this teacher had written nothing in the critical incident file at all. When asked why this was so, she replied 'Because nothing has happened yet'. Over the two weeks we had looked at a number of examples of critical incidents, and we had gone through a number of different ways of creating critical incident file items; but this teacher, who had been teaching what was considered to be a difficult split-grade mixed-ability class full-time over the whole period, had noticed nothing which she considered to be worth writing about. This was a very successful teacher for whom the classroom had become so utterly routine that she was teaching on autopilot. Her problematic was entirely practical, but there were so few practical problems, or they were so trivial, that they went entirely unrecognised. The entry, 'John didn't finish his work again today. Must see he learns to complete what he has begun' was in fact, the very first entry in this teacher's critical incident file, and only produced because I suggested that she write then and there about something that had amused or annoyed her and she chose the latter.[6]

Although the support group thought at first that it was rather an uninteresting, bland and simple statement, we found it took more than an hour to deal with it in terms of the four questions asked above. The group demonstrated that teachers have no difficulty with that kind of analysis though they had never before been asked to look at teaching in that way. And even if they had, none of them would normally have been able to find the time to do so: they were, after all, teaching full-time and completing part-time further degrees in education.

What made this case particularly interesting was that the teacher went back to systematically observe the pattern of events which led to John not completing his work. The first action plan was thus how to collect more data, not how to solve the problem in practice, which represents a significant move from the practical. Careful documentation of this case showed that the teacher was preventing John from starting anything new until the work begun had been completed. Talking around the question of why it should be completed we formulated the problem thus:

In everyday life outside the classroom we continually leave unfinished what we have begun, so how is it that we enforce upon these students the rule that they must finish one thing before they can go on to the next? Where did that rule come from? Why and when is it necessary?

All the teachers in the group realised that the rule came from themselves – it was part of their professional habitus and taken to be necessary in default of their never having asked themselves whether it ought to be as it was. Working this through, however, they saw that it was a largely unnecessary imposition coming from their own experience of schooling as well as from other agents and social structures, such as their principal, superintendent, scheduling practices, the students themselves and probably the community at large. The teacher decided that the rule she was using was not only unnecessary, but actually counter-productive in that people should be able to make a number of different starts in order to discover what they are good at, what they enjoyed doing, what they need to be able to do, and so on. So the second step taken in the subsequent action research was that the requirement for John to complete all his work and to do it in a particular sequence was lifted, and the effects monitored.

In the event, John turned out to be a boy who was not so much 'plain lazy' as easily bored. He had discovered that if he did not complete the work he began at the beginning of the day, then not only did he not have to do anything else for the rest of the day, but he was not even allowed to. So he sought all sorts of devious ways to entertain himself which he found more interesting than trying to complete set work that he had earlier lost interest in. This finding itself was generalised by the group to other questions about the hidden curriculum and correspondence theory, such as the recognition that in their classes students learned to time when they finished their work precisely so that they struck a balance between not finishing it (and having to complete it in their own time) and between finishing it too early (and then not having done it as well as they might, being bored or being given more).

And on that last point, this example is a good illustration of the way in which critical incidents can be used to effectively link theory with practice because one is working in the context of real and immediate practical concerns. On the one hand, school–work correspondence theory was seen to be relevant to that teacher's practice because the situation which it could be used to inform was perceived by the teacher herself.

But the most important point grasped by all the teachers in the group, was that what we thought was a good answer to this teacher's practical problem was in fact quite different to the one originally sought, because, as is so often the case, the situation turned out to be far more complex and value-laden than it had at first appeared. The answer lay not in finding a means of making John finish his work, but in a means of balancing what John had to finish (because it was necessary for him to have done or learnt a particular piece of work), with what John could leave unfinished, thus enabling the teacher to use the stimulus of a new activity to keep him interested in working.

CONCLUSION

I have spent time on this example because it provides an illustration of what is meant by theorising routine practice in order to improve it. Collecting and analysing data, examining values, planning a different approach, are all predominantly theoretical research activities, yet they radically altered what that teacher actually did in the classroom by altering her view of the location and construction of the problem. So a valuable outcome of this incident was that it clearly demonstrated that theoretical analysis, so often disparaged by skilled practitioners, actually led to a better practical solution: an important attribute for any theory, and essential for educational theory in particular.

But something yet more important than finding a good problem solution also happened: in questioning where such values came from, the teacher had to face not only her own habits, but also the contradictory and hypocritical way adults demand that children be made to do things they themselves cannot or do not do; how in such ways school becomes more a place for enculturation than instruction; and how schooling thus becomes separated from the lived experience of the society it serves. These ideas are clearly of a socially critical nature. In facing them and seeking answers the teacher was brought into contact with Rachel Sharp and Maxine Green, Michael Apple, Henri Giroux and others who have described and theorised class-room teachers' far from latent ideological and culturally reproductive role. Such understanding is clearly crucial to the personal and professional development of the teacher, and hence to education in general.

In this way we can see that answers to questions asked by way of theoretical analysis are logically the basis of action and have the power to radically transform it through a transformation of the actor's awareness of the situation. In such ways teachers can simultaneously begin to question and act upon their habits and the often self-imposed constraints upon their actions in their own classrooms. Critical incidents are an excellent means of setting a practical agenda; they facilitate problematisation through rendering into anecdotal form otherwise unremarkable aspects of teaching practice and enabling teachers to work on their own concerns. They can then use action research to change their classroom practice to align it more closely with the way they come to view it. The coupling of these two frameworks for thought and action can thus be seen to provide a potent tool for critique and change of the autopilot routines which so often pass for successful practice.

Finally, I would like to note that the analysis I have offered in this chapter is but one way of addressing the politics and contradictions inherent in the nature of eduction as a university discipline that arise from the fact that so many academics work primarily with the theories of other disciplines rather than with the actual practice of educators. Until we can show that we do question the operation of our own professional routines, we can hardly ask teachers to listen to our theorisations of theirs.[7]

Chapter 2

Interpretation: Creating critical incidents

INTRODUCTION

Most of this book exemplifies the use of critical incidents. In general, I find they have two major uses: they are an excellent way to develop an increasing under-standing of and control over professional judgement, and thereby over practice; and they are also a means of finding a focus for classroom action research. Unfortunately it is not possible to deal with this second use here, though critical incidents are constructed in the same way for both uses.

In this chapter I want to concentrate upon the nature of teacher's professional critical incidents, dealing particularly with the importance of diagnosis and how it can become an approach to teaching in its own right. Interpretation is important because we act according to what we think things mean. It is also the process by which we render incidents into critical incidents. In Chapters 3 and 4 I shall then outline some techniques which teachers and researchers have found useful for analysing incidents. And in the fifth and sixth chapters I shall deal with how to handle a collection of critical incidents by constructing a critical incident file.

WHAT IS CRITICAL ABOUT A CRITICAL INCIDENT?

The term 'critical incident' comes from history where it refers to some event or situation which marked a significant turning-point or change in the life of a person or an institution (such as a political party) or in some social phenomenon (indus-trialisation, a war or some legal negotiations). Being major events, this kind of critical incident occurs so rarely in a teacher's lifetime that it alone could not constitute an adequate basis for a professional research file, particularly one that is being used to inform on-going educational action research. But highly significant events (see, for instance, Incident 53: *Spitting* or Incident 49: *Homework*) do occur and have very important consequences, and so that is one kind of incident which ought to be included for professional reflection in a critical incident file (see Woods 1992 and 1993 for an account of this kind of critical incident).

The vast majority of critical incidents, however, are not at all dramatic or obvious: they are mostly straightforward accounts of very commonplace events that occur in routine professional practice which are critical in the rather different sense that they are indicative of underlying trends, motives and structures. These incidents appear to be 'typical' rather than 'critical' at first sight, but are rendered critical through analysis. An example of this kind of critical incident has already been presented (Incident 2: *Settling down 2*). It was an incident which passed entirely unnoticed when it occurred, but which was made into a critical incident by what was subsequently seen in and written about it.

There are thus two stages to the creation of a critical incident: first, some phenomenon is observed and noted, which produces a description of what happened. This could be called the production of an incident, which can then be explained (so we have 'what' and 'why'). The critical incident is created by seeing the incident as an example of a category in a wider, usually social, context.

For example, this observation is an incident:

Incident 8: Permission

Mary raised her right hand. After about a minute her teacher noticed, and asked her what she wanted. Mary asked if she could sharpen her pencil.

It is a description of what was observed. It is not an explanation because it does not say why this exchange took place at all. 'It is the way children are supposed to ask the teacher if they can do things' explains it, and 'Mary is conforming to the rule' tells us what is signified by it. But all this is still at the concrete level of the particular incident. To create a critical incident one would have to say what the incident meant, which means moving out of the immediate context in which the incident occurred. For instance, one might see that raising her hand to ask if she could sharpen her pencil meant that she was not allowed to decide such matters for herself in that class, and that in turn was indicative of the power structure of the classroom: it was one that made her in some respects dependent upon the teacher's rather than her own judgement and authority. And of course, Mary's classroom is contextualised by the school system which is contextualised within the local district which is contextualised within the wider national society. At each of those levels, the significance of the original incident (Mary raised her hand) will become more general: Schools teach children to accept and depend on the authority of the state rather than on themselves and their own initiative.

I have tried to schematise one way of creating a critical incident in Figure 1. Perhaps the most obvious thing to note about this is that there is a sequence to the analysis: it is only possible to suggest what an event means if we know what the event was (i.e. if we have described it). Similarly, it is only possible to find a more general meaning if we know what it means in its specific context.

It is also an important aspect of professional practice to act from a considered and justifiable values position. In this case, both the explanatory and the critical questions should enable us to arrive at a position such as, 'I think students should

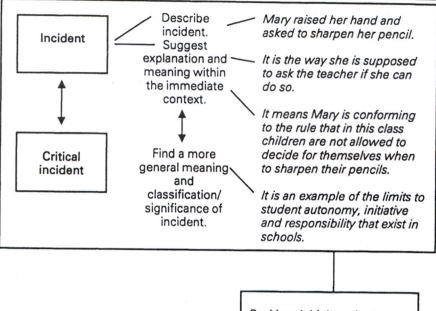

Figure 1   Creating a critical incident

be more responsible for their behaviour in school' which may well then make a teacher decide to let children decide for themselves when to sharpen their pencil.

Another feature shown by the figure is that 'the analysis' actually consists of several different kinds of analysis. All analysis involves breaking a complex structure into its simpler constituent parts in order to better understand its nature and composition, and what kind of analysis one uses depends upon what aspects one is interested in understanding, which in turn depends upon the purposes of the analysis. In Figure 2 I have named the kinds of analysis that I have used here according to the kinds of information that I want, and hence the kinds of questions that I would ask about the incident. I have then grouped these kinds of analysis into four sections because they are associated with different kinds of professional judgement which I have called practical, diagnostic, reflective and critical. These terms are dealt with in more detail in Chapter 9. In each kind I have emphasised the importance of considering the people involved.

I recovered these kinds of analysis from an examination of my critical incident analyses. I use the terms for the four kinds of judgement also as superordinates for the kinds of analysis involved in producing them, talking about 'diagnostic analysis' for instance to refer to the co-ordinated use of descriptive, causal, effectual,

Kind of judgement	Kinds of analysis		
	Information required	Questions asked	People involved
Practical	Procedural	What should I do? How? When? Where?	For and/or with whom?
Diagnostic	Descriptive	What happened?	Who was involved?
	Causal	What made it happen?	Who acted?
	Effectual	What does it do?	For whom?
	Affectual	What does it feel like?	For whom?
	Semantic	What does it mean?	To whom?
	Explanatory	Why did (does) it occur?	With whom?
Reflective	Personal Evaluative Justificatory	Do I like it? Is it a good thing? Why?	Do others like it? For whom?
Critical	Classificatory	What is it an example of?	Whose classification?
	Social	Is it just?	For whom?

Figure 2   Kinds of judgement and analysis

semantic and explanatory analysis. Of course, it is not possible or necessary to get all that information about every incident: some will be more appropriate than others depending upon the incident and the purpose of the analysis. As this book demonstrates, I do not take these questions as a formula, though to use it as a list of suggestions may help when learning to create critical incidents.

Returning now to our original point, Figure 1 shows that the incident itself (Mary raising her hand) was not 'critical' in any way in the context in which it occurred; on the contrary, it was wholly routine. To be critical, it had to be shown to have a more general meaning and to indicate something else of importance in a wider context. Thus one can see that critical incidents are not simply observed, they are literally created.

Just to expand on that idea, the point is that incidents only become critical because someone sees them as such. This is really just another aspect of awareness that was dealt with as 'problematic' in Chapter 1. We always operate with a habitual view of what is critical and what is not. Most of us would see an incident in which the roof collapsed or a student swore at us and overturned a table as critical because they are so entirely contrary to our ideas of safety and how students should behave in class. But if we expected roofs to collapse and thought such student behaviour was OK and it happened every day, we would not see either incident as 'critical'. Thus it was that the teacher who always had one music prize for the girls and another for the boys did not see her giving my daughter the girls' prize as critical in any way. On the contrary, it was a normal part of her routine. It was only when the child's response was analysed in detail that it became clear that the event was significant and should be questioned.

The point is that everything that happens is a potential critical incident: we just have to analyse it critically to make it one. The counsellor officer who tends to sit in the same place (in front of or behind his desk) when interviewing parents, can consider the effects on any routine interview. The adult literacy teacher who always asks students to write about themselves first, can consider that with reference to an individual or/and a whole class. The Deputy Principal who keeps staff informed through general notices and personal written notes, can analyse that. The teacher who likes to 'have a laugh' with the students, can critique that.

Those kinds of routines are not single incidents, but are nevertheless composed of a succession of them. A teacher who habitually brings her students out to sit on the mat at the front of the class when she wants them all to listen to her, and sits them at their tables when she wants them to write, has a routine. But that routine is just a repetition of what is, to all intents and purposes, the same incident, and the routine can therefore be critiqued in exactly the same way as can a single incident of things happening according to that routine. Because critical incidents should question the way things normally operate, those which deal with the minutiae of routine practices are therefore by far the most common, and the majority of the writing is subsequent analysis rather than dramatic narrative accounts of exceptional events.

DIAGNOSTIC TEACHING

One of the problems of presenting a method is that people may be left with the impression that they have to do all or none of it. This is not the case here, for there are many different ways in which critical incidents can be used on their own in everyday teaching. The skill of diagnosis is one of them. I want to show here how the analysis of critical incidents tends to produce an approach to classroom teaching that one might broadly term 'interpretative'. This term is to emphasise that professional judgement is based upon a scholarly analysis of our ideas of the meaning of the incidents rather than on our experience of the incidents themselves. The main reason for using 'interpretation' to make this distinction is that it indicates the construction and choice of meaning, and it therefore appropriately carries the idea that a transformation of experience occurs when one renders teaching practices into discourse.

'Interpretation' also seems appropriate for the creation and analysis of critical incidents in teaching because of its associations with what is often called the interpretive approach in the sociology of education.[2] Interpretive sociology aims to produce micro-analytic accounts of the everyday in terms of how participants receive, perceive, create and negotiate their 'reality', which is precisely what one does in the analysis of critical incidents. The point is that how one acts in an incident, what one learns from it and the judgements one makes about it, all depend upon interpretation. To explain this it is necessary to look rather more closely at what is meant by interpretation in the context of an approach to teaching. There are many different kinds of interpretation, but I want to illustrate just one interpretation, 'diagnosis'.[3]

It is unfortunate that diagnosis has associations with disease, because in its wider sense 'to diagnose' means, 'To identify by careful observation', a diagnosis being a 'distinctive characterisation in precise terms' (Oxford English Dictionary). But diagnosis also involves explanation by inference: one looks at the physical manifestations (or 'symptoms') and infers their causes. To term a high temperature 'a fever' is not a diagnosis; to see that a fever is being caused by flu or malaria is; identification of the disease through inference from the symptoms explains the occurrence of the fever. Accurate diagnosis is so important in medicine because it is a serious mistake to treat the symptoms of the disease rather than the disease itself, or to treat the wrong disease.

Diagnosis works in much the same way in teaching and is just as important. One can call one's interpretation 'a diagnosis' when there is reason to be relatively sure that one has identified the cause or causes of a phenomenon. Consider this incident:

Incident 9: Bad behaviour

Matthew kept messing around in our silent reading period, fidgeting, getting up, talking to himself and others. I'm fed up with his bad behaviour. Telling him off doesn't work for long. I'm really going to try to do something about it next time.

To term 'talking during silent reading' 'bad behaviour' is not a diagnosis; and to treat the 'bad behaviour' without trying to discover its causes can be both ineffective and harmful. Yet, contrary to medicine, lack of a diagnosis or an incorrect one seldom shows in teaching because it is possible to treat the symptoms with apparent success. The difficulty is that punishing a student for bad behaviour does usually make the bad behaviour disappear. But if the bad behaviour is in fact an understandable response to an underlying problem, it is a symptom of a problem, not the problem itself. If the student is then punished for the bad behaviour, the symptom will often disappear but the original problem may be compounded, perhaps with the addition of carefully hidden resentment. Thus traditional approaches to discipline often mean that suppression or transformation of the symptoms of underlying problems that may be preventing learning is actually seen as successful classroom management. That view may account for diagnostic expertise not having become a professional ability generally expected of teachers.

Another reason that teachers are not taught to diagnose their practice is that the difficulty of diagnosis is immeasurably greater in teaching than in medicine because students can choose which symptoms to display, when and where and to what degree, and even whether to display any symptoms at all. This means that symptoms of a problem may or may not be made manifest to the teacher, and that if they are, they may be made to appear in quite different ways by different students, and in different ways by the same student on different occasions.[4] This is very important because it means that accurate observation of phenomena alone is not a sufficient basis on which to judge the best action to take. As in medicine, what teachers do should depend more on their understanding of the cause of a phenomenon than on the manifestation of the phenomenon itself. Which is the reason for dealing with incidents critically.

Tempting as it is to see diagnosis as an objective matter of facts, it is important to remember that all diagnosis is interpretation, which means that one has to construct and choose a meaning from among several possible meanings.[5] These aspects are well-displayed in the 'translation' of languages: interpretation is necessary because the equivalent words of different languages do not have precisely the same meanings.[6] So in teaching, interpretation is necessary because there is never a single way to categorise an incident, action or situation. It is a characteristic of the professions that interpretation is something each member does for him- or herself, even if the judgements of colleagues are sought and taken into account. Interpretation is also a matter of one's taking a 'position' on something. 'We interpret this as a threat', is an interpretation because we acknowledge that it may not have been intended as such and that others could see it differently. What interpretations we make are therefore very much determined by who we are. It is for that reason that it is so important to reflect upon and critique our judgements.

In fact, interpretation is essential to professional practice because it always comes between observation and action. One student is copying from another: what the teacher does depends entirely on what he or she decides the act of copying means for those children in that situation. If it were during a test, the teacher would probably interpret the copying as 'cheating'. If the student who was copying had missed the previous lesson, it would probably be interpreted as 'catching up'. If the students were working together on a project, it would probably be interpreted as 'collaboration'. And so on. Because in each case interpretation has involved seeing the behaviour as an instance of a particular category, it is a diagnosis, though which category is chosen does not depend upon what is happening (copying), but upon an understanding of what the student is trying to achieve, the history of the incident, its current context, and so on. Those things are a fairly straightforward factual matter involving description. And, given sufficient information, one could easily match the description to a general category to make a diagnosis.

Again, diagnosis in teaching is in this respect more complicated than in the practice of Western medicine because some diagnoses themselves require interpretation.[7] Suppose, for instance, that an incident in which one student copying from another was diagnosed as cheating, the reason for the phenomenon (copying) is explained, but by a phenomenon which itself requires explanation: what caused the student to cheat? That is a much more difficult matter which may well stretch the professional resources of a child psychiatrist to understand and explain. So the teacher has to make their own judgement, which will depend very much upon how well they know the child, how they regard cheating, and their understanding of the situation in which it occurred. Their diagnosis is a matter of their understanding of the meaning and significance of what they observed: they may decide the copying was an aberration for a usually honest student; that it was simply too easy to copy; that the student did not regard it as important; that it was the result of too much parental pressure; that the student was over-anxious to succeed; and so on. The only way to decide why the cheating occurred is to analyse the incident as much as possible, making a judgement based upon an interpretation of the meaning of cheating in the incident. For such reasons, diagnosis, though an essential tool, should be seen as a specific kind of a more generally interpretive approach to critical incidents. Diagnosing a critical incident is one way to ensure that our reflection and evaluation is grounded in actuality.

THE DIAGNOSTIC TEACHING CYCLE

Being aware of what something means to us is of little practical value unless we do something with it. Creating a critical incident before acting in or analysing an incident is a matter of postponing action and reflection, not of avoiding them. One way to use critical incidents in our practice is to follow some kind of an action research cycle such as in Figure 3. In this strategy one alternates between action in the field of practice on the one hand, and interpretation in the field of discourse on the other. Reflection is centred on a series of incidents, each of which is explained prior to action, the explanation then being used to inform the response to what happened. In this approach, the teacher keeps a critical incident file in which incidents are first of all described and then analysed. These incidents then act as both an agenda for further action and a way of evaluating and interpreting it.

This cycle can be used instantly during teaching in an informal way. But when it is used in the more formal way described here, there may be a delay of anything from a day to several weeks between making an observation and responding to it. This is not just because interpretation based upon scholarly analysis takes time; it is also because it has to be worthwhile investing the effort necessary to create critical incidents, which means that the matters that arise in the incidents tend to be large and important ones.

DESCRIBING INCIDENTS: THE IMPORTANCE OF DETAIL

Moving on to the recording of incidents, I will also continue to indicate further aspects of the nature of critical incidents as we look at how to create them. As usual,

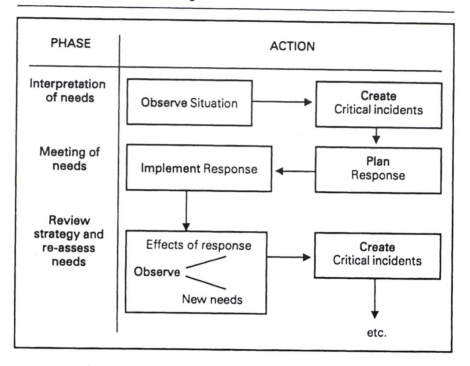

Figure 3   The diagnostic teaching cycle

I will exemplify points with actual incidents, mainly those described by teachers with whom I have worked over the past few years.

Most critical incidents begin with a concrete description of an event, or idea. Detail is a primary characteristic of incident descriptions because, when one is dealing with meaning in the wider contexts of a critical incident, one is inevitably dealing with generalities. In any case, critical incidents belong to the research journal tradition, and a fundamental characteristic of journals is that they should be more elaborate than a diary. I take that to mean both that critical incidents should be more detailed than diary entries, and a critical incident file should be more systematic. These are two basic criteria of quality, and as will become apparent, they are cardinal in determining the usefulness of a professional critical incident file. It is important to conceive detail and system as emerging, developing and continually shifting attributes, for it is neither desirable nor possible to have such qualities in every part of a critical incident file right from the outset: files need to be made to become detailed and systematic. Very few critical incidents will be 'fair copy' or 'final draft'; as in journals, the main characteristic of critical incident writing is lack of closure and continual revision. In fact, many of the entries will be actual events rather than critical incidents, simply because critique is a much slower and harder process than description of an event. Detail is important precisely because it is important to have detailed and accuracte incidents available for critique.

Leaving the matter of system aside for the chapter on the structure of critical incident files, detail in critical incidents tends to be developed in two different ways: through focus and enlargement. Focus is clarification of the whole picture by increasing the definition of the existing details to make it all clearer; and enlargement is changing the size of the things in the picture so we see more of the picture in less detail, or less of the picture in more. The former process is generally termed 'progressive focusing', the latter, to continue the photographic metaphor, 'cut back' and 'zoom'. The more one can emphasise both of these aspects of detail, the more comprehensive the final account of a phenomenon. Note how in interpreting Mary's hand-raising, 'cutting back' to include the broader context was essential in rendering the incident critical. But more detail is necessary to validate the interpretation that all the children in the class have to asked to sharpen their pencils: we need to 'zoom in' on that aspect of the incident to make sure that it is not just Mary who has to ask (because she makes a mess).

The value of developing detail is well-illustrated in the following incident description:

Incident 10: Teaching rooms

Delamont proposes that the classroom setting and personal front has a bearing on how students assess their teachers as individuals. She compares the two Latin staff and suggests because one of them is consistently moving around the school and is not in one particular room, then this teacher is supposedly unorganised and not really on 'permanent' staff. I have found, in most Western Australian schools especially in senior high schools, you tend to get moved around a fair bit and unless you are in a specialist area such as science which requires certain forms of equipment then you expect not to have a permanent room as your base. This is often unsettling to students and most importantly to first-year out teachers who find it very much a disorientation.

In terms of the language (including constructions) this is typical of an initial incident description. It is not a 'bad' entry, for it is not possible to make such overall judgements. Critical incidents are more or less useful with regard to particular purposes. The purpose here was to generate a personal response to a research paper (Delamont 1976), which the teacher, having read, was then applying to his own classroom. In terms of professional development, the aim was for this teacher to think about his practice through making case to case generalisations. Inasmuch as he draws upon his own experience to exemplify Delamont's observation, it is a useful entry. As it stands, however, the picture presented lacks sufficient detail for any other interrogation to occur: there is very little other than the bare statement that he has had a similar experience and so he is endorsing Delamont's point. But as the quality of a critical incident can only be judged according to the use to which it is put, the entry is quite effective.

However, if the teacher wanted to inform others about the matter, a more detailed and methodical kind of observation would be required. This could be done by 'zooming in' to enlarge upon some aspect of the picture, such as, for instance, on the teachers' responses to moving classrooms in terms of their use of resources; or the students' responses in terms of their sense of belonging to the school. We need some actual 'for instances'. The picture could also be made more 'focused' by clarification of what 'disorientation' actually means to him, or of just how much movement is involved in his teaching day. That should probably include examples of the effects of the teachers' being moved around, so the reader would know the kind of data upon which the judgement (that it is bad) was made.

The language of the original entry reveals where more precision in the recording of observations already made is required: words such as 'often' are used when it should not be difficult in this case to make an attempt at deciding how often, when and why. Observations (such as 'This is... unsettling to students' and 'Teachers... find it very... disorientating') remain merely personal judgements unless supported by actual incidents. To judge the validity of this teacher's opinion we need to know the ways in which and occasions when the phenomena ('unsettlement' and 'disorientation') do or could occur.

Having revised the entry through the addition of such information, the teacher might then use it with colleagues and students in order to discover their reactions and experiences. That information could then be used to further revise the entry, but it could also be used in other ways, such as in the design of a questionnaire on the matter to inform school policy.

We can now see why it is not possible to judge entries without regard to the purposes we wish them to fulfil. Simply to tell us nothing more than that his own experience makes him agree with Delamont's point, is a valid purpose for an entry, and it serves that purpose well. But if the teacher wishes to do anything other than register his opinion of the matter, then he will have to include a great deal more empirical detail to provide the reader (who may still be only himself) with a far clearer view of the whole picture.

With regard to methodology, this example shows how zoom and focus are progressive processes: one can always return to further develop an entry. One of the differences between the two, however, is that focusing normally occurs more or less constantly and evenly with each theme or issue as the teacher clarifies their observations and ideas and the way they express them. Cut-backs should also frequently occur as we should always be able to see an incident in its wider (social) context. Zooming, on the other hand, occurs spasmodically as enlargements are only necessary when a particularly useful or interesting facet needs to be verified. The point of the photographic metaphor is that one improves the actuality of an incident by 'focusing' and 'zooming' in on its details; and one makes it critical by 'cutting back' to see how it is significant to wider social contexts.

Overall, then, the main point to remember is that it is only worthwhile providing very detailed descriptions for incidents that are important to us, and which we are going to analyse in some depth. So many incidents will and should remain 'notes towards an entry'. This means that it is not possible to say how much detail is necessary in critical incidents: we can only ask, 'Is this incident described in sufficient detail for me to analyse it in the way I wish?' As we shall see later, it is surprising just how much even fairly simple methods of analysis can produce from a few details.

NOTICING CRITICAL INCIDENTS

Attributes of events

Bearing in mind that many teachers, when they first embark on a diagnostic understanding of their teaching, have some difficulty in deciding what incidents to record for further analysis, it helps to use some techniques to assist observation. Most people find that the analysis of events is the best way to begin, and one of the easiest ways to generate critical incidents is to look for certain adjectives one could apply, such as interesting, funny, sad, silly, witty, violent, unfortunate, boring or good. If a teacher goes into a class having decided beforehand to make a note of anything funny or fortuitous which happens, they actually alert themselves to be more receptive to a whole range of incidents, because it is necessary to canvas everything in order to select the funny or fortuitous. The very act of deciding beforehand what is to be looked for, forces the question 'Is this what I'm looking for or not?', and to answer it one has to examine the whole range of incidents in order to discount most of them.

One particularly useful adjective is 'trivial'. Incidents which we recall only to dismiss as trivial are often a good indicator of criticality because the very fact that we have recalled them means that there is probably something important about them, something which has made them salient for us in one way or another. But it is our very judgement of them as trivial which can be a way by which to deceive ourselves into thinking we can legitimately dismiss them, when we should actually consider them in great depth. A good instance of that kind was Incident 7, about the boy who did not finish his work. In that case, the teacher at first refused to share the incident with the group, because, 'It's too trivial'. Another example that came in response to my asking a group of teachers to write about 'something trivial' was the following:

Incident 11: Getting started

I have this child in my class, Kate, who won't start what I've asked the class to do until she's called me over to explain some silly little thing. No sooner have I finished my instructions than up goes her hand. It really annoys me sometimes.

It did not take long for the group to suggest that here was a child who needed some kind of help which the teacher hadn't been giving. Various hypotheses were put forward, such as, attention-seeking behaviour, lack of confidence, anxiety (to please, to get it right, to win, etc.), learned helplessness, lack of prior concentration, and inability. As we talked the matter over, the teacher clarified for herself that she probably over-emphasised the need to do things exactly as she asked, and she began to work on reducing dependency and increasing initiative and variety in her students' work. What had become salient as an emotional reaction (annoyance) but was ignored because it seemed so petty, became a matter of professional judgement and deliberate action. The matter was always there, it just needed to be exposed, which it was by looking for something that was thought to be too trivial for consideration.

Typical/atypical events

Another very straightforward way to generate critical incidents, is by looking for examples of two classes of event: those which we can term typical, and those that appear to us to be atypical or even unique. The second category includes events which appear to be counter-instances and exceptions to rules. Typical events are when something happens which the teacher expected to happen because it seems to them to be always happening. Incident 38, about the fact that students never seem to follow instructions in examinations, is a typical event.

Such events are worthwhile recording and then analysing in order to see what it is that tends to produce the event. Four possibilities are (a) that a particular sequence of events always precedes the typical event (trend or pattern); or (b) that a particular person is always involved in a particular (perhaps catalytic) way; or (c) that the incident always occurs in a particular relationship, when certain roles are played, or (d) that there are always certain constraints such as time, place, expectations, aims or demands.

Atypical, unique events, exceptions and counter-instances, enable one to work the other way round, by asking why an event is uncommon or why it did not happen as expected. It is often said that the exception proves the rule (because something can only be an exception if there is an already existing rule), so in a real way exceptions may be used to formulate and verify rules.

Examples of rules and exceptions could be the very routine aspects of running a classroom, such as asking for quiet in a particular way and getting or not getting it; speaking to a particular child in a particular way and getting a particular response; noting one's movements in the classroom, and looking for a factor which would explain why, at a particular point, the teacher was standing behind the desk rather than, for instance, at the back of the room.

Then there are the class rules themselves. The way in which these are implemented can be a rich source of exceptions.

Incident 12: Manners

We had been working on manners. I had suggested a few very basic ones, the first of which was knocking before entering the room. To encourage the students I had a daily 'Good Manners Award'.

After lunch on the day we started it, the first visitor was the Head. He just walked into our room without knocking, interrupting me to check on something (irrelevant) and Chris yelled out, 'He can't get our award. He didn't knock on the door, or wait till you had finished speaking.' How true. The kids thought they were wonderful picking someone up, but the principal didn't seem to appreciate it all that much as I did.

He shuffled out of the room and left me to explain that perhaps we might add to our list of good manners that we wait until the visitor leaves the room before we comment on their manners.

An amusing incident, though one which caused both teacher and principal some embarrassment. It is interesting how often, as soon as an apparently simple rule is set up to follow in school, the rule merely proves the world to be more complicated than anticipated. In fact, 'good manners' does not mean that everyone behaves in the same way. Manners are primarily codes by which we express relationships, particularly status, and are thus contingent upon power. There is nothing absolute about manners: doing or not doing something does not mean it is good or bad manners, but depends upon the people and the context. It is a good illustration of the point that only certain people are bound in certain ways and certain occasions by classroom rules, so all teachers have to constantly make exceptions.

Manners are a constantly repeated concern of teachers, but because there is no substantial and commonly available research on how children learn manners in different settings, or on how they may be taught, this entry on its own is difficult to analyse much further. But we can cut back from the particulars of such an incident to the underlying and more general social processes that are operating, by considering whether there is another (contradictory) rule of which this incident is an example, not an exception. Here, we know, for instance, that there is a nexus between privacy and intimacy, and status and power. In the school context, the degree of intimacy and amount of privacy depends upon status, bestowed by institutional role, which is hence a feature of power. This is clear when one considers that in this school, the Principal may go anywhere without knocking or waiting to speak, the teachers may go into most rooms in the school without knocking (though not into the Principal's study) and generally wait to speak, but the students may go almost nowhere without knocking and must always wait to be asked to speak.

We do not know much about what markers of power there are in our schools, how they support or contradict each other, to whom and in what ways they are beneficial or harmful, or whether there are procedures and rituals which teachers could and should operate upon. But once we have understood the general social significance of one such incident, it is possible to return to the specifics of our practice by seeking other examples of the same general rules. These are often found in conventions such as modes of address, control of discussions, or allocation of tasks. The point is that incidents become critical incidents when one tries to explain an incident by locating it in a wider context, in this case, by forming a general rule from a single incident. One should always modify and verify the rule through searching for other examples of and exceptions to the rule.

Vicarious experience and research reports

Another way of generating critical incidents is to compare others' experience to our own, which is something we actually do quite naturally all the time. Staffroom discussion of a class or student generally consists of comments about their behaviour (appearance, personality, etc.) as they are with us, and we usually find that the behaviour varies considerably from class to class. This pooling of such experience may lead us to observe our own situation more carefully, to revise our opinions and judgements, even to behave differently ourselves. Such casual and specific comparisons are often too limited and unsystematic for the researching teacher, who needs to consider the broader implications and to collect more and better information. So one way to broaden and verify our experience is to compare it with the results of published research findings.

This is basically a way of linking theory to practice: we can read articles and then go back to observe our teaching looking for evidence as to whether the (necessarily generalised) conclusion of the article is true in our case. Whether it is true of our practice or not, we need to create data about the ways in which it is or is not true in order to explain why it is so. A teacher can read an article, on, for instance, competition and co-operation (Johnson and Johnson 1975), and then look at their class to see how these strategies are (or could be) used by him- or herself and the students, collecting some incidents to record in their critical incident file and using them for further analysis. Here is an example of my own thinking deriving from published research in this way:

Incident 13: Air pressure

Barnes (1969) shows how students don't so much just work together as work 'off' each other in the sense of learning occurring as an (inter)active social encounter between people who remain individuals.

When his students were looking at air pressure, he found that it was 'the social processes' which contributed most importantly to the level of understanding reached: without Steve's help, Glyn would not have represented to himself so clearly 'what made drinking possible'. This is obviously a very different dimension to group work from Britton's (1969: 98) 'group effort at understanding'.

In my STAR tutorial, I think I am managing that aspect OK, because they seem to pool their ideas well; but I think now I have also to enable them to use the group to clarify and develop their own individual understandings and insights more. I think that occurred in Barnes' case because of the task: air pressure is not ultimately a matter of opinion and consensus like my group discussion topics. I need something more specific, and I think I'll try to look at defining some of the concepts like 'ideology' and 'culture' that we're using.

That entry is the result of reading some of the published literature and generalising it to my own practice. Note how it is possible to transfer the main idea (of socially mediated individual learning) from a science topic with school students to a history of ideas course in university. As I suggested earlier, there are difficulties with this approach, but when it does work it can be a very simple and efficient way of initiating observation and change.

From reflection to incident

In all the incidents we have considered so far, an incident has been recorded and then analysed. But very often we find that we have reached some kind of a conclusion in our thinking without having recorded or noted any actual instances: they have occurred, but the separate incidents have disappeared into a general sense of knowing. As I suggested in the example of Mary raising her hand, we often find we are acting from a value position which is not actually based upon the facts. We then need to examine our practice for data that will confirm, modify or challenge our existing values position. This means moving from a conclusion to data rather than the other way around. It was partly for this reason, and partly because we should consistently check our conclusions against the data, and re-analyse the data, that the relation between an actual event and a critical incident is shown as a two-way interaction in Figure 1.

The following entry is typical of someone thinking through an evaluation in the absence of any actual incidents.

Incident 14: Labelling

What is of some concern is having the labels of ESL and Remedial attached to the one teacher. I know the administration made the decision for the one person to do everything for economic and financial reasons, but I wonder what impact this has on the perceptions of students, parents and staff. Is a message being given that students from non-English speaking backgrounds are somehow less able than their monolingual counterparts?

When asked whether there were any incidents that might answer the question, the teacher could not think of any, but subsequently she observed one student ask another if they were 'spastics' because they were in a remedial group. This did not so much answer the question asked as pose another: did the very practice of withdrawing children for special attention categorise them as different and inferior regardless of the label attached? Both the research and further observation suggested that this was so, with the result that the idea of changing the labels was dropped in favour of pushing the administration to allow all children at some time to be withdrawn for 'extension'.

So one can usefully work from analysis and questioning back to an incident, and in so doing, may change the conclusion previously reached. This process is a form of exemplification which is important in all theory building.

Re-reading incidents

Finally, a very important way of generating new critical incident file items is through reading earlier entries and writing about them.

Incident 15: Wilful blindness

I've just finished re-reading what I've written so far this term and what surprised me was how often Malcolm was mentioned. I didn't know I'd written about him much at all, and in one way I haven't: not one entry is devoted to him. But I've highlighted his name wherever it occurs in all the other entries, and it does in over a third of them! When I look at why his name occurs, it is always in the context of something bad: he can't keep control; he 'borrows' without asking and then doesn't return things; he doesn't do his programmes... and so on. I've been studiously ignoring the fact that Malcolm is involved in almost every incident I've written about. I'm now going to have to do some really deep thinking about him and our work.

The importance of re-reading is that it enables us to see such patterns and trends as they begin to emerge. If you look at Incident 26: *Reading 26 July*, you can see how the matter of reading was the real problem, though it was initially seen only as a symptom of difficulties in the children's attitudes and discipline. Looking back and realising that it was problems with the teaching of reading that caused the other difficulties, the teacher was able to regard herself and her teaching ability quite differently: she was not an incompetent disciplinarian, but lacked experience in teaching reading with an age group she had not taught before. Further discussion of this process of re-analysis occurs in Chapter 7 with regard to personal professional histories.

CONCLUSION

In this chapter I have tried to show how it is the unremarkable and everyday events that make up our routine professional lives that are often the best indicators of the patterns and values that underpin our practice. It is through rendering critical the incidents of normal everyday events that much personal–professional development can occur.

Although I have drawn attention to two different kinds of incident in this chapter, the division between the two is, of course, not often clearcut. Seldom does one produce an entirely 'uncritical' incident, though I have taken some trouble to show that these are important in their own right. Equally seldom does one analyse a critical incident as far as one can, drawing from it all possible social significances. Most critical incidents are somewhere between these two extremes. As I showed, one begins to move from description when one asks questions about an incident and one often sees a single aspect of a deeper meaning indicated by it, without following all its ramifications through, or looking for other meanings.

In conclusion I would like to return to the idea that one of the occupational hazards of being a successful teacher in a system during a period of little growth or change is to become captured by one's own routines. Although routines are essential to all professional practice, when they dominate they can often make us lose sight of what we are trying to achieve. Punctuality, for instance, is a necessary routine, but Peter (of 'Peter's Principle') once found a manager who so insisted that his buses would always run on time that drivers were not allowed to stop to pick up passengers if they were running late. Less obviously contradictory, an important routine in creative writing is for children to draft their work; but always to insist on multiple drafts eventually reduces the number and type of pieces attempted. Recently, I made the following entry about a routine in my file:

Incident 16: Explaining readings

Still having real trouble getting the first years to do the reading. Before the lecture I gave them a quick seven-question test on the chapter on morphology I'd set them to read. 84 per cent didn't know what morphology meant; 19 per cent couldn't spell it. We talked it over and they said they weren't doing the readings because they were so difficult that they couldn't understand them and they got the main ideas from my lectures anyway. 'How do you know,' I asked, 'if you're not doing the readings?' In fact I don't cover all the main points in the lectures, so how can I help them to do them?

I decided that as the reading–lecture–workshop sequence I had always used was not working, I would try a lecture–reading–workshop sequence, using the lecture to reduce the difficulty of the reading and find workshop activities for which they would have to have done the reading. In terms of the number of students doing the reading, it worked much better.[8]

So teaching routines are essential, but to keep them successful, we must constantly challenge and monitor them. One of the aims of incident analysis is to scientifically and systematically initiate, assist and record the process of developing personally and professionally as a teacher. The point is that committing any incident to paper enables the writer to reflect upon the experience, and thus gain much more from it than if it were simply to pass unremarked and unconsidered in the routine of teaching which we constantly need to vary, develop and adapt to suit changing circumstances. To create critical incidents enables us to become aware of things we otherwise take for granted. And, having written them down we can then show and discuss that record with others, such as a teaching or research partner.

Of course, the methods described here of generating critical incidents are only some of the ways into the 'genre', and should not be taken as a closed formula for creating them. As outlined in Chapter 5, critical incidents should grow and develop a life of their own as themes emerge and our perception becomes more focused and controlled. But when one is well into the diagnosis and evaluation of professional practices through critical incidents, such methods are still useful as ways of opening up our minds again, so that the critical incident file does not become too narrowly focused on known issues. And one way of doing that is to take a new look at our routine practice.

Chapter 3

Four approaches to the analysis of incidents

INTRODUCTION

In analysing events to create critical incidents, we are usually trying to confirm (verify) something we already suspected (hypothesised), but analysis can also reveal something entirely new. Whatever the outcomes, thorough, systematic, accurate and clear analysis is essential to good professional practice because diagnosis and critique questions what is, and enables us to think of what might be.

As I suggested in the previous chapter, I find the simplest technique available for analysing incidents is to ask a series of different kinds of questions. In this chapter I want to go on from there to outline four other methods, all of which are more structured, even to the point of appearing to be rather algorithmic in style. Like all algorithms, there is a danger of over-reliance and mindless application, though they need not cause such problems unless they are the only kind of analysis done, or are treated as immutable 'right' ways of analysis. To the contrary, these methods are nothing more than a systematic way to begin: where the final analysis goes and what conclusions are reached should vary according to the intentions of the analyst and the nature of each case. We looked at the uses of different kinds of questions in the last chapter, and here we look at four other methods: thinking strategies, the *Why?* challenge, dilemma identification and personal theory analysis. The next chapter then deals with a fifth approach, ideology critique.

Before dealing with those techniques, however, I should make something of a confession: until recently I had always stressed that the single most important aspect of teachers' professional critical incidents was that they were for their own use. Recently, however, I discovered a contradiction: that whenever I have written a critical incident that I have found really useful, I have gotten as much excitement from sharing it directly with others as I have from the insights and understanding that I have developed for myself through writing it. I discovered that, rather than writing for myself, for myself I write for others. And when I reconsider the entries that I have included here, I can see that whilst I was enlightened by writing them, my enlightenment also enables my teaching of others.

Needless to say, when I reflected upon this phenomenon I found some aspects very worrying. In particular, when I looked at the teachers' critical incidents contained in this book, I saw that the majority had been encapsulated within my writing: very few were left to stand entirely on their own. In one sense, I am not overly concerned that I had done that, for in creating critical incidents about teaching critical incident creation to teachers, it is inevitable and appropriate that I should use their work. What really did concern me about the course I was running, however, was that I was asking teachers only to write for themselves. I had thereby so limited the teachers' purposes in writing that I was in fact denying them the very purpose that I found most rewarding in my own work, namely writing for others. It was for this reason that I made it a course requirement that at least one critical incident was sufficiently developed so as to be suitable for publication. These critical incidents were then collected and circulated locally.

I learned two important things from this experience. First, many of the teachers found that they shared my paradoxical experience: that it is in writing for others that we learn most and gain the most satisfaction from our learning. Second, we found that the requirement to develop an entry for publication was an excellent way of learning how to write critical incidents: the discipline of anticipating what others would need to know, how they might react, what they could criticise, and so on, was an enormous stimulus to thoroughness in terms of precision, detail and the consideration of alternative hypotheses and points of view.

Bearing in mind, then, that perhaps the best way to learn how to create critical incidents is to write for others and to share one's writing with them, I have found the following suggestions helpful in getting started.

THINKING STRATEGIES

Thinking strategies are perhaps the most straightforward and least personally challenging method of analysis, but they do offer a process that helps frame the kind of questions that will begin to produce a deeper reading. Strategies are also useful in counteracting our habitual ways of thinking about things. For instance, one I often use I call non-events.

Non-events   The fact that one thing has happened always means that some other things have not happened. But when something happens we tend only to ask why it happened; we do not naturally ask why what did not happen did not happen. Yet seeing what did not happen often reveals the significance of what happened. Asking what Mary did not do instead of asking the teacher if she could sharpen her pencil, shows the effect of the rule.

Making a note to ask that kind of question of an incident is a kind of thinking strategy. There are a number of different collections of thinking strategies available, but I find de Bono's (1987) 'CoRT Thinking' programme the most useful, partly because it has the added advantage of being packaged for use with students, which means one can also use it to elicit their view about what is happening in their classes. I find the following processes of the de Bono programme to be particularly useful, but I summarise them here simply as examples of the kind of strategies that are available.

(a) Plus, minus and interesting   Every situation or new idea has both good (plus) and bad (minus) points about it; there are also points which are neither good or bad, but simply appear to be relevant to the situation (interesting), such as new ideas sparked off by the original. Looking at an incident in this way also gives an idea of the general position taken, for it is a matter of viewpoint whether a particular point is classified as good rather than bad, or vice versa. Clarifying what we like or dislike about an incident is both a good way of evaluating it and how we relate to it.

(b) Alternatives, possibilities and choices   There are always alternatives, though we don't always bother to create them. As the pro-active side of 'non-events' deliberately thinking of other things that could have happened and devising ways to make them happen is the creation of choice.

(c) Other point of view   There is always more than one point of view, and it is important that we deliberately seek out other views, particularly those of both participants and informed non-participants. Generating another point of view is a two-stage process: we need first to analyse what we expect their point of view to be, and then we need to check it out with them. Very often the difference between the two will be most illuminating of our own assumptions and opinions!

(d) Parts and qualities   Amongst all the ways of looking at something, two would seem to be most basic: we can look at it as a collection of parts, or we can look at it as a set of qualities. For instance a bicycle can be seen as wheels, handle-bars, chain, etc. and it can also be seen as red, fast, non-polluting, dangerous, expensive, liberating, etc. Modern Western rationality typically makes us break things down into their component parts and the relationships between them, without either our seeing that a structure amounts to a great deal more than the sum of its individual parts, or our examining our feelings and attitudes towards it. Because teaching is a social practice, we must examine our attitudes, values and judgements and work on those too.

(e) Reversal   The opposite is always a possibility, whether it is looking at something from the opposite point of view, or simply turning it on its head. This can be a particularly challenging form of analysis, because it produces a new alternative for consideration. For instance, a teacher wrote, 'I cannot do drama with that class because I'd lose control'. Two rather different reversals present themselves: 'I can do drama with that class because I won't lose control', and 'I will do drama with that group because I'd lose control.' Both reversals shift attention from why we could not do something to how we could do it. It turns a justification for inaction into questions about it:

- How will I handle losing control?
- How will I regain it?
- How could I do drama without losing control?
- What kind of control would I be losing, and what other control could I replace it with?

Whether to do something or not is the basic dilemma of all our teaching decisions. The above example is merely a version of what may be said to be the fundamental curriculum question, namely, 'Should I not do that with this group because they cannot do it? Or should I do that with this group because they cannot yet do it?' Deliberately reversing our habitual answers to such (often unasked) questions, is a very powerful form of challenge.

(f) Omissions   Finally, it is important to check our analysis of a critical incident to try to find out what we may have left out. Of course it is never possible to be sure that our thinking is complete in the sense that we have thought of everything, because we do not know what we've not thought of till we have thought of it, in which case we haven't not thought of it! But the point is we often tend to stop analysing as soon as we have understood one aspect, which is too soon in the sense that we have not considered all possibilities. So it's often useful to re-work an incident to see if we have considered all the ideas about it which we are capable of generating.

THE *WHY?* CHALLENGE

Another simple form of analysis that can be far-reaching and sometimes quite devastatingly dramatising in its effects, is, like Socrates, to ask, and go on asking, the question, *Why?* When we do this, we do not go on for ever, but we may go on for a long time before we find that underlying our action or idea is one of two things: a normative statement or some form of reification. In effect the end point is the same: we see that things are as they are because we choose to make them that way. In practical terms, if we ask *Why?* for long enough, we end up saying either, 'Because that's how it ought to be.' or, 'Because that's how it is.' In the former we have to recognise that we are operating from a deeply held belief which may or may not be appropriate to our work or consonant with our other beliefs; and in the latter that something we take for granted and as a part of the natural order of things and therefore unchangeable, may in fact be a social construct and therefore open to change. Either way, it is our responsibility. Different kinds of ideas and actions tend to go in different directions, and at certain points will often require something more than a plain *Why?*, such as *Why does it matter?* The following incident was handled in this way:

Incident 17: Plagiarism

Several of the students have taken my ideas from the readings and extensively used them in their essays. They've all acknowledged that they have used my work, but in none of the essays is it clear exactly where my ideas end and theirs begin. Is this a form a plagiarism? I'm not sure, and neither am I sure that it matters greatly to me: I'm pleased (and perhaps a bit flattered) that they have found the ideas useful. But the University has the most draconian rules and punishment for plagiarism. In the end I decided that what they'd done was typical of much academic practice: when we write about an idea we tend to acknowledge who else has dealt with it, but, unless we are simply citing the idea and the associated name, we often select only the bits we want to use (which may be a misrepresentation) and add our interpretation to the rest. In fact, we often just cite others who have had something to say on a matter to justify our own ideas on it. So why is plagiarism so important?

My first attempt at answering this question was as follows:

Why?
Because it's cheating.
Why?
Because it's not their work.
Why?
Because they've copied someone else's work.
Why?
Because they want to pretend it's their own.
Why?
Because they want to get out of doing the work or get a better mark.
Why?
Because a mark is an indication of how well you've done.
Why?
Because you have to have measures of how good people are, and that's one
    we happen to use.

But answers to *Why?* do not necessarily follow one path to a particular conclusion, particularly when we feel free to vary the straight *Why?* with something else. So a second questioning of plagiarism went as follows:

Why?
Because it's cheating.
Why?
Because it's not their work.
Why does that matter?
Because it's stealing.
Why?
Because it belongs to the original author.
Why?

Because when someone writes something it's theirs, it belongs to them.
Why?
Because that's the law.
Why?
Because it's only fair, that's all.

And we are back to a different value. In contrast to those outcomes, we could take another incident as an example of something that ended up as a reification:

Incident 18: Silent work

A teacher in my Wednesday group complained today that he could not get his 9-year-old children to stop talking while they wrote. 'What do you mean by not talking? Do you require all talking to cease?' I asked, 'Of course.' 'For how long?' 'About 20 minutes.' I asked why they had to write in utter silence for so long. He thought I was joking, so I asked him to tell me why.
Why?
Because you can't concentrate when you or others are making a noise.
Why?
Because you keep looking and listening to what the others are doing.
Why?
Because it's more interesting than writing, and not such hard work.
Why?
Because writing is less interesting than talking to people and it's hard work.

I chose commonly enforced rules in schools and colleges for these last two incidents. In the first case it becomes clear that plagiarism is wrong because it invalidates the competitive system of assessment which we have to have (normative statement: only because we believe it is necessary); and in the second case, that writing is necessarily less interesting work for students than talking (reification: only because we make it so). Note how the answers can include both normative statements and reifications; the *why?* challenge exposes both of them, making what has been clarified open to critique.

Looking at the two examples in practical terms, many teachers would wish to work on the matter of how to make writing more interesting; not only does it have more immediate and personal rewards, but it is also a great deal easier to change one's students' attitudes to writing than it is to shift the whole educational system away from competitive assessment, or to change the copyright laws. But that does not mean that questioning the last two ideas is not worthwhile: the more frequently and the more different ways in which it is raised, the more conscious of an issue one becomes. One does not have to disagree with something and wish to change it to make critique worthwhile: having worked out for oneself why it is that one believes something should be so makes one more committed to the position. Building and clarifying rationales for professional judgements is an important form of personal–professional development.

DILEMMA IDENTIFICATION

Incident 19: Non-communication

A teacher has a child in her class who will not talk to any adults in school, including in class; she won't even reply to a question requiring a single word affirmative. She'll talk to other children, however, and they talk for her. Either she tells them what she wants them to say, or they offer suggestions until she chooses one with a nod. On the one hand, the teacher could see that everyone could get along perfectly happily in this way, but on the other, she could see that the child would never learn to talk to adults or in public unless she were made to in one way or another. Any pressure in the form of attention or encouragement appeared to increase her withdrawal from communication. The problem was whether to intervene or to leave her alone.

It is surprising just how often incidents contain teachers' dilemmas, and it is important to recognise them as such for two reasons. First, recognising what may appear to be just another uncomfortable situation as a dilemma enables one to deal with it much more clearly; second, it is important to realise that the source of the discomfort is not due to any shortcoming of the teacher's, but is created for the teacher by the dilemma. I strongly recommend Ann and Harold Berlak's book, *The Dilemmas of Schooling* here, because their classification of dilemmas offers a very straightforward but powerful way of analysing and understanding certain kinds of incident.

Just to outline very briefly what they mean by teaching dilemmas, in their studies of teachers in England in the early 1980s, the Berlaks realised that the great stress of teaching comes both from the number of decisions teachers have to make every minute and from the nature of the decisions they have to take. Teaching decisions are, by and large, matters of choosing between mutually exclusive options; what they choose is a matter of professional judgement. A teacher cannot both intervene in and ignore a situation, for instance; nor can they always treat a child both as a whole person and as one of a group of learners; nor can they treat all students exactly the same and allow for individual differences. Teachers have to do one thing or the other, and a single decision may involve the resolution of several such dilemmas, which is necessarily very wearing and stressful.

The Berlaks, like others, point out that overall the schooling process contains a number of major contradictions which amount to what might be called an 'omni-dilemma': by taking control of the children's lives away from them, schools are supposed to prepare children to take control of their own lives. From this come other dilemmas, such as that teachers are expected to make children independent learners and thinkers by teaching them a prescribed curriculum of prescribed 'correct' answers; or that they are supposed to use extrinsic rewards and sanctions to develop intrinsic motivation. Behind all these dilemmas is the matter of control. As Barnes had put it a few years earlier:

At the heart of teaching as we know it in our culture lies this dilemma: every child learns best when he is finding out about something that interests him; children are compelled by law to attend school, and are in the charge of teachers who are employees responsible for large numbers of them. There is an implicit conflict between the teacher's responsibility for control and his responsibility for learning: the one treats students as receivers and the other treats them as makers.

(Barnes 1976: 176)

It is the way in which the aspect of control is inherent in and realised by the schooling process that is theorised by the Berlaks:

The dilemmas are intended to formulate the range of tensions 'in' teachers, 'in' the situation and 'in' society, over the nature of control teachers exert over children in school.

(Berlak and Berlak 1981: 135)

They divide these dilemmas into three sets and show how dilemmas often overlap more than one set, particularly how curriculum dilemmas have a social dimension, and *vice versa*. The point of their list of dilemmas is not, of course, to be able to classify a dilemma one has already recognised, but to check a situation to discover if any dilemmas are present in one form or another. The following is an example of an incident where the teacher thought that, however good her reasons, she had simply chosen the wrong option.

Incident 20: Star students

Katherine has always been by far the best student in her French class, but she has come to see me after the lesson, at recess-time and twice at lunch-time to ask me questions on the past tense – why wasn't she able to ask these questions in class? Her explanation was that she thought she understood in class, but then afterwards she realised that she wasn't really sure. In fact, although she made a few minor errors she really had grasped the basics – so why keep coming to see me?

Hypothesis   Her 'position' in the class is being threatened by Sharon – the new girl who is better at grammar and who is able to answer every question correctly. Katherine wants to understand and learn everything, but won't ask questions in class because she sees this as an admission of ignorance, leading to a loss of face.

Inadvertently, in fact, I have exacerbated the situation in that I deliberately made a fuss of Sharon, asking her questions, praising her, etc., because I wanted to make her feel that whilst the lessons may seem terribly simple and perhaps boring to her, she is, in fact, playing an important role in helping the others in the class to understand the work, whilst she revises.

Towards Katherine, on the other hand, I acted as I have always done, expecting her to know the answers and acknowledging the fact that she can cope perfectly well. On the rare occasion when her grasp of the concepts wasn't quite right, I explained her mistake, hoping that the others who were experiencing real difficulty might be encouraged by thinking that even the best students can ask for and receive help. In doing this, however, I heightened Katherine's awareness of her threatened status.

As suggested above, this example contains several dilemmas, most obviously whole child versus student, individual versus social learning, equal versus differential allocation of praise and attention, common culture versus sub-group consciousness. It is highly unlikely that any teacher, however experienced, would be able to get the balance between all those considerations exactly right from the start, especially considering the fact that Sharon was relatively unknown to the teacher. What is revealed when one looks at this as a dilemma, is not that the teacher had done the wrong thing, but that both the two right things she could have done had inherent detrimental side-effects. If she ignored Sharon's advanced knowledge of grammar, Katherine may have been less threatened but Sharon would have been bored and felt unwelcome; but if she used Sharon's knowledge, Katherine's self-esteem would suffer. The teacher really needed to find a non-threatening way of using Sharon's ability. This she did by continuing to ask Sharon orally, whilst asking students to prepare set grammar exercises, at which Katherine could shine too. Seeing it as a dilemma not only helped to clarify the situation and indicated the kind of resolution necessary, but it also enabled the teacher (and the present reader) to see how well she had done in such a difficult situation.

PERSONAL THEORY ANALYSIS

I use the term 'personal theory' here to refer to an articulated set of beliefs that informs our professional judgement and thereby our action in the material world. In this next example I want to show how values, as one set of beliefs, influence our judgement. Dilemma identification is useful here, because why we chose one resolution rather than another enables us to identify the values inherent in our professional judgement. Because underlying values are always present, they have already appeared in a number of incidents; but the following incident has been chosen to illustrate the way in which the choice of one dilemma resolution rather than another depends upon unstated values, how a set of values acts as a theory, and why it is important to analyse an incident in more than one way.

Incident 21: Waste

Whilst on duty I have noticed fairly frequently one girl continually putting her food into the bin. The child looks around to see if anyone is watching and if not, quickly pops the lunch into the bin. The first few times the incident was overlooked or ignored but it being constantly repeated is causing me concern. The child is clearly being 'sneaky', so the problem is how to correct the whole situation rather than just make her devise more sneaky methods of lunch disposal.

Action   A lesson on the importance and care of food was given in today's social studies lesson. Groups were set up to discuss amongst other things, wastage of food. The child in question was made a group leader to report group's findings. Her group's findings sounded very convincing but must wait now for practical outcome.

An obvious dilemma here is 'the child as person versus child as student', not just whether to enforce the rule or not on this child (which this teacher has not done before now), but how to do so. Because one uses professional judgement to resolve a dilemma, recognising the values that inform our judgement is one way of understanding why we resolve a dilemma in the way that we do. Here there are a number of values embedded in the teacher's account of her action amongst which are the following: that knowledge affects values and values affect behaviour; that teachers can and ought to transmit values, particularly those enshrined in rules; that knowledge of values is best achieved through peer group exposition; that children will find 'the right' values for themselves when correctly 'set up' to do so, because certain moral imperatives are correct conclusions of rational discourse; and that procedural rules are legitimated by self-evidently 'right' moral values.

Taken together, these provide the kind of explanatory and predictive power of a theory. It explains the relationship between morals and rules, and how children best learn them, but it's not a public, empirically based theory: it's more an account of how this teacher sees the world. As such, it's private, discursive, constructed and coherent, and therefore a personal theory. It can even answer why the child would not waste food knowing it was bad to waste food though she would break a school rule knowing she should not.[1] Being a theory it is a complex web of ideas which includes a view of the nature of children, namely that children are less likely to break a procedural rule if they understand it as a moral imperative. In commenting on this incident to the teacher who wrote it, I did not disguise that fact that I had different values, but because there appeared to be no conflict between the teacher's personal values and her professional judgement, neither were they my concern.

What did concern me was that I felt the idea that children are simply 'sneaky' misinformed her professional judgement about what action was best for the child's long-term well-being. Sneakiness is a 'black box' term (like 'the weather' or 'dyslexia') which labels, but does not explain. I do not believe that children do 'sneaky' (meaning 'sly, deceitful, underhand') things just because they are inherently 'sneaky'; my experience is the opposite: children are naturally honest and open about what they do till they discover things they have to hide from adults. Children generally have good reasons for breaking such procedural rules, but because they cannot change the rules and are punished if they are caught breaking them, they are forced to hide their rule-breaking, as this child did. The child's behaviour was not autonomous, but a direct response to what was being done to her. Children have all sorts of reasons for not eating the lunch they are given: they do not like it but are not able to say so or are ignored when they do; it does not match up to their friends' lunches; they really are not hungry at that time; they are given too much, and so on. But because the idea that children are intrinsically sneaky explained her behaviour, it obviated finding out why the child actually behaved as she did.

Theories about children that prevent interpretative teaching are potentially abusive and professionally dysfunctional, and I felt moved to say so. I said that not telling the child that she had been observed breaking the rule or that the lesson was meant to change her behaviour, was in itself 'sneaky', and that I considered the idea that if a child eats food they are thereby not wasting it, irrational in any case. In discussing my views with the teacher it became clear that, although at a conscious level of thought she was merely reporting what she was doing, at a deeper level she had reported it because she was disquieted about it and knew she needed to reflect upon it. It was for her a disorientating dilemma of the kind that Mezirow (1981) suggests are a necessary precondition for critical self-examination. What she could not see by herself and at that time she recorded the incident was that she had reason not to be entirely happy about the incident. Thus, contrary to the negative impression that one might have received from my analysis of one aspect of her theories, this is a picture of a thinking teacher who is sufficiently concerned about what she is doing to commit it to paper, and in so doing to expose her very self to critique. That process is highly professional.

Such an example also shows how the dilemma decisions teachers make are as much based upon their unarticulated personal theories as upon outside constraints of the exigencies of the situation. There was a school rule that children must eat their own lunch, and not swap or dispose of it, so the compulsion to be a good teacher and enforce the rules was as strong as the sedimented value that eating everything that you were given to eat, even when it was more than you wanted, was good use of food. And these also conflicted with a number of other wholly laudable desires that informed her action:

1   To enable the child responsibly and independently to transfer knowledge from formal school learning to her own behaviour.
2   Not to embarrass the child in front of her peers.
3   To offer the child the opportunity to make up her own mind, rather than simply being told.
4   Not to make it a disciplinary matter, perhaps involving the parents and others.

So what appeared at first sight as a merely practical dilemma (to intervene or not) soon showed as one that went right to the heart of the theories upon which this teacher's professional judgement was based. Her articulated aims were undermined by an unrecognised, taken-for-granted idea. Teachers have to take hundreds of decisions of such complexity every day, and just how they balance one factor against another to form a judgement and act upon it, depends upon their theories. Critical incidents can reveal these theories, but at the same time may also expose contradictions existing within and between different components of each theory, and between the theories themselves.

Overall, then, this example shows how even a very obvious dilemma such as whether to ignore rule breaking or enforce the rule is situated in a whole series of highly complex practical, theoretical, and moral judgements and decisions. Dilemmas unmask such problems and it takes a great deal of courage to face and deal with them openly.

CONCLUSION

As the next chapter continues the theme of this one by outlining another approach to analysis, all I would say in conclusion here is that all the critical incidents thus far show just how essential it is not to base global judgements of a teacher's professional competency upon a particular analysis of a single incident. In this last incident, for instance, how could anyone condemn the teacher's action, when, as a general rule, it is in the child's interest for the teacher to help her to change her own behaviour through helping her to change her ideas about the world? Certainly it is preferable to changing the child's behaviour by enforcing rules. Because there are always competing interests and values, it is seldom if ever possible to get everything entirely right in any one instance, let alone all the time.

Many times a day in their work teachers experience the feeling that if they had done what they chose not to do, things might have turned out even better. But they can never know for certain. That is one of the very stressful and often demoralising aspects of being a thinking, feeling teacher. The value of critical incidents is that they can reveal how the habits we have and the tendencies we form influence aspects of our teaching, thus increasing our understanding of our practice and informing our actions. Without knowing who we are and why we do things, we cannot develop professionally.

Chapter 4

Ideology critique in the analysis of critical incidents

INTRODUCTION

I have devoted a separate chapter to deal more fully with ideology critique, because ideology critique is fundamental to professional judgement in that ideology itself is inescapable; all we can do is to choose what ideologies we wish to adopt. Further, as a procedure, ideology critique is extremely productive: I recently read a 30-page analysis of the text of a lapel badge (Frow 1983). Although it is probably necessary to say something about the concept of ideology here, there is such a vast amount of literature on the topic that I do not pretend to have achieved any kind of a full summary even of my limited reading. What I want to do is to introduce some of the main ideas about ideology, and to explain some of the key terms one finds in the literature. I shall illustrate each theoretical point with a concrete example.

First, a simple definition of ideology that makes its importance to professional judgement clear is that it has to do with the way in which certain ideas represent the world to us and make us think and behave in certain ways. Many of those ideas are quite explicitly and consciously subscribed to, but are nevertheless pervasive and persuasive. For instance, a belief that life on earth is but a preparation for a longer life that extends beyond (but not before) it, will make people consider it wise to behave in ways that they would not consider wise if they believed that life spent on earth was the only form of existence. It makes more sense for a believer in life after death to seek martyrdom, for instance, than it does for someone who believes that death terminates existence.

Unfortunately, ideologies are usually more complex than that, because many of the ideas according to which we think and act have been instilled into us without our active participation or learning, and often without our even realising that we have accepted them. Thus, in a society in which all land is owned freehold by someone, few people will realise that individual land ownership is not necessary or natural, but is simply a way certain societies have found for organising and legitimating its use. Although a number of land-occupying people may realise that freehold land ownership is but one way of enabling people to occupy it, few will question whether it is a good idea, fewer still will formulate alternatives, and almost no one will operate according to an alternative.

Ideologies are such ideas: they legitimate what we do or is done to us by others, and they inform our judgement about what is normal, necessary and right; though they are often irrational, they act as rationales for the behaviour of individuals, groups and institutions. It is because we are subject to various ideologies that scholars tend to see and refer to people as 'subjects', rather than as free individuals; and it is because people are instrumental in regulating the behaviour of others according to ideologies, that people are also referred to as 'agents'. Women who believe that children are best brought up by their mother are likely to either bear children or have a career, but not to do both at once. Their behaviour is determined by their ideas about what is best and right. These subjectivities (such as what someone thinks it is to be a parent) are thus ideologically constructed and maintained. And because people's behaviour is subject to an ideology, inevitably they become agents of it: consciously or unconsciously, they act as approved or disapproved examples to others, or advise them on what to do and why.

Ideology's main function in society is to legitimate (or to explain to people's satisfaction) the way things are, especially when things are not to people's satisfaction. 'We cannot pay ourselves more than we earn', says the politician when defending wage restraint. Most workers agree with the 'logic' of the idea, and so accept a falling standard of living. 'As a registered welder I am not able to sharpen drills', says the employee, and the employer accepts the idea of speciality, and employs an engineer to do the job.

But ideologies also work at a hidden and unarticulated level, presenting one thing as another: as I write this, everyone in Australia, employers, employees, politicians, commentators, is talking about a national 4 per cent pay rise in return for productivity increases. The fact that there is an annual inflation rate of over 8 per cent, however, means that a 4 per cent 'increase' of wages in cash terms is, after deductions, a 6 per cent annual decrease in purchasing power. The actual value of a wage is not how big it is, but what can be purchased with it; because the value of wages is always presented as the amount of money received, it is possible to talk about a real wage decrease as an increase. Similarly, a productivity increase actually means working harder. An accepted way of thinking about wages has turned 'working harder for less money' into what I have heard people talk about as 'their' pay and productivity increase. Ideology is thus often associated with the suppression and distortion of ideas, or with 'false consciousness', as it is called. False consciousness is most frequently applied to a situation in which subordinated groups or individuals do not recognise how they are being manipulated and oppressed because they think about themselves with ideas that are supplied to them by their oppressors. Thus it is that people will accept what is actually a wage cut if they think about it as a wage rise.

Six characteristics of ideology

Ideology is about much more than simple false consciousness, however, and it is necessary to make just a few more points very briefly to fill out the notion. Point one, ideologies do not spontaneously arise and autonomously maintain themselves: they are socially constructed and maintained, and they serve the interests of certain groups in society. Clearly the ideas of the rights of inheritance of goods and the rewarding of mental labour more than manual are not the only ways we could organise things, nor are they equally advantageous to all members of society.

Two, ideologies are not monolithic, which is to say that they are never fully integrated, seamless and independent wholes. Ideologies always contain (and exploit) contradictions, they have many different and distinct parts, and they connect with and depend upon each other. Business people who espouse a market economy will complain about health and safety regulations as government 'interference', but expect the government to protect them with tariffs, to subsidise a national minimum wage, and to prevent monopolies. Similarly, those who demand a close correspondence between school and work, expect schools to teach students to work, but not also how to avoid working.

Three, because a powerful ideology is often referred to as being 'dominant', people tend to think that it is irresistible. But ideologies are never without opposition, resistances and alternatives. They are dominant in the same way that a tennis or squash player might be said to dominate the game when they win most of the points, but the winner may still have been strongly resisted throughout the game, and they will not have won all the points. Similarly, the dominant ideology of modern consumerism is that 'newer is better'; but that does not stop people buying vintage cars, collecting antiques or having car boot sales. Indeed, the used goods industries are only possible if people are continually replacing still usable with new goods.

Four, as that example shows, all power tends to create the forms in which it is resisted, and ideology, being a form of power, is no exception. Needless to say, that is very obvious in school: children who are taught that work is something that one does in silence, immobile and alone, will resist work with noise, movement and communication.

Five, and further to the last point, the more detail in which an idea is spelled out, the more easily it is resisted, and the more obvious are the methods of resistance: if a requirement for each student to do a piece of work on their own is specifically made, students are not only tempted to ask 'Why?'; they are also alerted to the fact that it is much easier to do it together (for if work could not be avoided by collaboration, it would not be necessary to make that particular requirement).

Six, ideology itself is inescapable, but that fact does not mean that one cannot escape a particular set of ideas: one can always escape an ideology, but only into another. That's what makes ideology analysis so important: it makes us more (but never wholly) aware of what we do and why, and thus enables us to choose, control and modify the ideas that we wish to live by. Uncritically taking that very idea (that ideology critique is necessarily a 'good thing') is, of course, an ideology itself, and one to which many people do not subscribe. Judging those people to be evil, power seeking, unjust or just plain wrong, is another ideology. One can never actually 'touch bottom' as it were. So, ideological as it is, in teaching, ideology analysis enables us to make rational, informed and deliberate choices about our practice. Furthermore, by helping us to understand what happens to us and why, it enables us to act in an emancipatory way to improve the situation of subject people. Once we realise that we are operating a highly individualistic competitive classroom, we can choose to continue in the same way or to change it. If we are forced by an external examinations board into more competitive learning structures than we judge are conducive to learning, we know where and what kind of changes should be made.

The pervasiveness of ideology

This last point shows that, although ideology is not escapable, it is also very necessary: we could not do without ideology, because the ideas act as reference points by which we can make judgements about what to do. It is our ideology that allows us to decide what, in terms of social justice, is a 'fair' way of sharing scarce resources. Consider a simple everyday problem, that of having to share something fairly between several people because there was not enough for everyone to have as much of it as they would like. Apart from 'per capita' allocation (equal amounts to each person), so called 'fairness' of distribution can be achieved in at least the following twelve ways:

(a) to each person according to their 'needs';
(b) to each person according to intrinsic personal differences (merit/gender/ age/...);
(c) to each person according to extrinsic personal differences (status);
(d) to each person according to what they (say they) will do with it;
(e) to each person according to how much of it they've already got (per cent);
(f) to each person according to how much of something else they have already got (land, money, education);
(g) to each person according to what they have previously had (tradition);
(h) to each person according to what certain other people have (relativities/inheritance);
(i) to each person according to what they demand;
(j) to each person according to what they can take (power);
(k) to each person according to the judgement or preferences of the distributor;
(l) to just one person alone (lottery/ballot).

The point is that the twelve methods suggested are generated and informed by ideologies, so that whenever we use one of them we are in effect operating according to the ideology that justifies the method. As I said above, ideologies are not simple or coherent affairs, but one can see in broad terms that socialist ideology, for instance, would probably favour giving to each person according to their needs and to each person according to intrinsic personal differences (such as merit, gender or age). A liberal ideology would probably favour allocating to each person according to extrinsic personal differences (such as status), to each person according to what they (say they) will do with it, and to each person according to how much of it they've already got (as a percentage wage increase). A feudal ideology would think it right for each person to have the same as their parents had. And a free market ideology would tend to favour allowing each person to take what they can get others to give them.

Apart from the 'per capita' method, all the other ways of dividing something involve giving different amounts to different people which are all considered to be 'fair' by different people with regard to different things. What might seem surprising is that there are so many ways of achieving 'fairness' other than by 'equality'. So in the normal allocation of scarce resources, the way we often operate is to achieve fairness through unequal allocation. If, as I suspect they do, most people believe 'fair' always means 'equal', the term 'fair' will often effectively disguise unequal distribution ('It is only fair that the best business people should keep what they can earn.'). Second, the synonymy would tend to make people see a particular instance of unequal distribution as an exception ('You will never get everything fair for everyone'). And third, because each of these unequal methods of division is 'fair' according to different sets of ideas, attention is turned away from the idea of equality ('People should be given as much education as they can use', versus 'People should pay for their education', rather than, 'All people should be entitled to the same amount of education').

The example illustrates three ideas: first it shows how society could not function unless it were able to generate and use such sets of ideas. But second, that these ideas then pervade our thinking and tend to become uncritically accepted. Third, it shows how ideologies can control our behaviour by suggesting and favouring certain courses of action over others.

AN APPROACH TO IDEOLOGY CRITIQUE

There are many different approaches to ideology critique, but perhaps the simplest involves a sequential examination of at least four different aspects which can be done in the following way:

(a) Describe the phenomenon, and attribute meaning and significance to it in terms of the accepted (dominant) view.
(b) Analyse and examine that view for internal inconsistencies, paradoxes, contradictions and counter-instances, including what is being omitted from the viewpoint, the structured silences and absences.
(c) Look for reasons to explain why the dominant view (a) ignored or excluded what you found in (b); attribute agency, and suggest whose interests are best served by (a), and who is most disadvantaged by (b).
(d) Search for an existing or create a new alternative structure which is more rational and socially just than (a), by utilising what you found in (b) and (c).

Clearly, it is much easier said than done, so it might help to take as a very simple example the way I used the technique on the problem of why a teacher thought it necessary to make students finish their work, which was the example discussed in Chapter 1 (pp. 18–22). Working through it step by step, (a) first of all in the tutorial group, we analysed the accepted point of view. In it we found that making students finish one thing before going on to the next taught students to value products above processes, and to become obedient and diligent workers by finishing their work. These points I then tied in to correspondence theory in curriculum about school as preparation for employment and life as a consumer of products.

Under (b) we dealt only with the first aspect, for which the kind of inconsistencies to emerge were that the rule made certain students so bored that they actually did very little work, but learned more about how to avoid it. It also ran counter to methods theory that there should be variety in the class, and democratic notions about the rights of students to be treated as individuals to enable them to fulfil their potential, and to have some say in and responsibility for their own learning.

Thus it became apparent (c) that the reason for ignoring the way in which we operate in everyday life where we seldom finish what we have begun before doing other things, was because schools were seen to be places set apart from everyday life where, according to the current received view, different rules ought to apply. That not only advantaged teachers as the custodians of school knowledge and the arbiters and ministers of justice, but it also served the interests of future employers who could expect children to be thus accepting and docile workers. Those most disadvantaged were children who wanted to do things in their own way in their own time.

With regard to (d), the new structure that the teacher adopted was that school should be made to correspond more to everyday life outside the work place, and a more appropriate structure was one in which it would be legitimate to scrutinise and call into question certain classroom practices if they appeared to be counter-productive in the classroom, particularly with regard to certain students' learning, and run against the continuity between school and home so necessary for a secure environment. An obvious choice of an already existing alternative structure was a negotiated curriculum (Boomer 1982) in which a few tasks and activities were designated 'core' and 'essential', and the majority were 'open', where students could do as much as they wanted, or rotate between several different things without necessarily finishing each thing first, or indeed, at all.

It is very important to realise that there is not a single 'right' answer in ideology critique: it is necessary rather to develop a number of different readings. In that regard, it is obvious that we could have analysed the incident quite differently, perhaps from the point of view of a power struggle in which the teacher used that particular constraint in order to assert authority over a bored student, not in order to ensure learning about completion of work, but to prove to the student that teachers can and will make students do what they do not wish to do, or to develop perseverance in the student. One only has to choose between such different viewpoints, though not necessarily decide which is 'more correct', when action is to be based upon it. Any explanation which fits the data is a useful hypothesis worth exploring, and even if it is later rejected, it can be used again on another occasion.

One need not necessarily follow the four questions above, but they are there as a framework for raising the right kind of questions to expose ideology in a practice.

Incident 22: Mat time

(a) **The accepted view**   A traditional and accepted part of the pre-primary day is a time when teachers, children and usually helping parents gather together for the 'mat session'. A supposedly informal gathering, the daily mat session is valued as a strategy for socialisation of the group. In my case I use it to give the children practice in reading one another's names, to sing, do finger plays, action rhymes and dances. They all sit in a circle while this happens, having first found their allotted place in the circle by finding their own names on a card. The reverse side of the card has either their address and telephone number or a birth date and each child reads, or tells the information to me or a helping adult. Then we have 'news', a sharing time where a maximum of six children show and tell about something that has been brought in for this purpose.

It is a time for participation, for listening, for imparting 'gems of knowledge', a time to 'do something' about science and a great opportunity to have auditory and visual memory and discrimination games, and to work on everyday concepts. As long as it is kept moving along a lot of ground is covered. It is viewed by me as a 'teaching time' for the whole class. The rest of the day is perceived as 'interaction' time.

(b) **Analysis of the phenomenon**   In fact, the mat session has become a daily 'hurdle' to be jumped before I can relax and enjoy the day. It has been used by me as a useful vehicle to 'snow' the group with 'knowledge', get through the curriculum requirements in the shortest possible time, teach songs and finger plays and get the dancing done. It is supposed to be an exercise in socialisation for group awareness, but that means listen to me instead of talking to one another.

This is a power play. While paying lip service to treating each child as an individual in school, we first of all have our indoctrinational session of 'group-ism', so any individual who demonstrates individualism is brought to heel by the implicit parameters of 'group' interaction. *After* this session they are 'allowed' to be individualists, *after* the daily reminder of where they belong in the power hierarchy.

Individual children are assigned positions through the name placings and are expected to like the person sitting alongside, even if the normal pattern of interaction is to fight on sight. Free socialisation is not allowed, because everyone is learning to 'take turns', even in talking and answering questions. The person answering the question may not have a clue, but to call out the right answer is 'rude'. If you have something really exciting and interesting to show the group, you have to wait your turn (which may not be until Thursday) while another child shows the same boring old car they had before. The need to dance with the allotted partner, ostensibly for including the 'isolates' and shy ones, is really a strategy to separate the noisy boys and thus avoid the resultant chaos.

I often suffer feelings of guilt because the constraints of 'news giving' and showing things have eaten into the precious five minutes set aside for 'Where water comes from', or 'How people use (?abuse) the environment' and I know that the group are so bored and restless by this time we must do a dance instead to release pent-up energies. However, as well as releasing pent-up energies it also releases any vestige of concentration that was left and 'Social Studies/Science' must be deferred to another day because they have all been conditioned to expect 'activities' after dancing.

We usually end the 'mat session' on a note of mutual relief. I then break the group into smaller groups and interact individually on different tasks and be 'me' not 'teacher'.

(c) Rationalisation of the dominant view   The dominant view does not acknowledge the problems because there is covert pressure to limit the degree of individualism. Otherwise, why the need to take a group of innately individualistic and egocentric beings and stress the virtues of co-operation and altruistic behaviour? 'Treat each child as an individual' has been an early childhood slogan for years, but what about the hidden curriculum? At the end of the slogan is a silent 'within your system' as all teaching is encapsulated within a system of curriculum guidelines, physical and demographic constraints and the over-arching 'cultural umbrella'. We are becoming an increasingly multi-racial society, but those unfortunate Chinese or Vietnamese children must be part of this exercise in groupism so they more quickly learn the language and how to get along with Australians in Australia. All children must learn to 'get along with other children'. Be individualistic as long as you are also conforming, compliant and obedient.

Whose interests are being served? The teacher's, as this session gives her the 'stage' for convincing the captive audience of what is right and wrong and imparting 'knowledge'. It is a chance to quickly checklist cognitive skill areas and find who is and who isn't receiving the messages in this area.

The physical arrangement of the children in a group, or circle, sitting on the floor is a physical constraint through both peer conformity pressure and the teacher's position, in a chair, facing all the group. This places the child at a disadvantage both physically and socially. A single protesting voice is soon drowned in disapproval. If there is further resistance the ultimate weapon is used against them – the threat or act of withdrawal – being a pariah.

As the year progresses, these happy, outgoing and friendly little beings become so well indoctrinated to the norms of conformity that 'removal from the group' is accepted by almost all as the ultimate punishment. When it happens the other children are reminded, by implication, that they have failed their task of peer pressure.

(d) Some possibilities for an alternative I don't believe this can be changed within our existing schooling system because teachers do not really determine educational outcomes. Modifications can be made, curriculum changed, innovators can be heard, seen and publicised, but the educational process is still determined by societal forces and fiscal constraints. Schools are the most successful means of occupying our young for the required ten-plus years. Schools are staffed by the products of schools and almost every teacher has experienced the early socialising experience of 'the mat session', or an equivalent 'whole class' teacher directed learning and interaction session.

If we were to open up the system and allow each child to directly interact with the environment in a free and exploratory way, who would be used to monitor the process? Who would be on hand to mend the broken equipment, replace the lost puzzle pieces, clean the walls, tend the injuries and how many children would be allowed to attend such a free-for-all by their conventionally socialised parents who expect children to 'learn' at school?

Even if we found sufficient individualistic teachers to staff the centres, who will fund them? There are private systems, some community schools where the philosophy of individualised learning and freedom of action is encouraged, but these depend on parental support, both practical and financial. How many parents in the wider community would have the time, resources or interest to involve themselves in what they would probably perceive as a dangerous experiment with their children's future?

In spite of the shortcomings and limitations on personal liberties and individualism, I do not see any viable alternative to this type of group teaching for a short session in each day. As an exponent of the Vygotskian view, there is still a place for the teacher to teach, to act in a more affirmative role than a facilitator who structures a learning environment and hopes something will happen. Children have interacted with authority figures since birth; to them the schooling experience involves interaction with a different set of authority figures and same age peers – whatever the teacher does is accepted by them as the norm.

I can use the mat session for developing important cognitive and social skills, whilst maintaining a constant awareness of and receptivity to the problems. I must be flexible enough to modify and rethink the daily format when the session has become so routinised it is a bore for all concerned. In this way, by a process of evolutionary change, I can meet the changing needs of a group of individuals in the best interests of the group, even if not of every individual all the time.

That analysis is typical in that the end result was not to abandon the practice, but to seek ways of mitigating the problems inherent in it. It is a typical outcome because most practices of most teachers are valuable and effective overall. Of course there are dilemmas: if we decide that all children should speak to the group, we deny them the right of choosing not to. What the analysis does is to enable the teacher to decide where contradictions occur, how important they are, and what to do about them.

As one gains experience of this kind of analysis, one may find such a sequential approach rather too limiting. The last example in this section is a more critical analysis of a more traditionally ideological concern: the teaching of history. Here is a teacher using the questions in a fairly algorithmic fashion. They did not follow the algorithm step by step, but, having explored and challenged a certain practice, wrote in a more narrative fashion. It was written for two purposes: one to show the way in which the hidden curriculum is structured to reinforce certain cultural values; and two, to show how the analysis of incidents that happen within the confines of a particular lesson on a particular day with a particular teacher, have very general implications: it is a truly critical incident.

AN IMPLICIT HISTORY LESSON

Incident 23: Cultural history

In Social Studies we have just started a topic on Early Settlement in Australia. We started the course by looking at how Aborigines may have arrived in Australia many thousands of years ago. It was an interesting lesson judging by the number and form of questions from the children. Our next lesson was to do with early European contact with Australia.

This incident was written by a teacher in a remote, limited-access Aboriginal community. To an outsider, there is a values issue here which is very difficult for the writer to spot, precisely because, as a skilled and experienced teacher of the centrally developed state-wide syllabus, what is to be taught has been so taken for granted for so long. The crucial point is that, in the syllabus, the ratio of content about the coming to this continent of the Aborigines versus its colonisation by the Europeans, is about 1:9. That balance alone should make it very clear to the students what constitutes valuable and important knowledge in school because we tend to spend more time on things we think are more important. So the differential allocation of time probably teaches the students more about the value of their history and culture in a European's estimation than it does about their origins, which, anyway, is a much disputed topic only amongst Western scholars: all aborigines have their own accounts of their origins.

Elsewhere (Tripp 1991a) I have argued that curriculum, and hence the implicit (or hidden) curriculum, is systematic. Assuming that to be the case, we should be able to see aspects of the pattern of that structure begin to emerge through an analysis of incidents such as this one. Structural analysis means that we must regard any particular incident as an instance of wider attitudes and values, and not merely as an isolated and coincidental side effect of essentially neutral curriculum decisions. That means that we should find within this incident other aspects which reinforce a devaluing of Aboriginal culture. And when one searches the account, two fairly obvious aspects which appear to work to reinforce that attitude emerge.

First, there is the use of the single word 'Early' to cover, and thereby to bracket, both the Aboriginal and European settlement phases, which were in reality thousands of years apart. That disparages Aboriginal culture by implying that whatever happened between the two was of no historical importance. Second, and this point is really an explanation of the first, by dealing with the event of settlement rather than with the routine of life, history is portrayed as consisting of a collection of corroborated facts about unique people and events. This may not seem remarkable, but it does account for the 'non-history' of the Aborigines in European scholarship. A major effect of a factually constructed history is that the more unique people and events there are, the more potential history there is. A largely oral culture which emphasises the unchanging nature of its traditions, thereby has no 'history', because each year of the lives of each generation has been much the same as every other throughout the millennia. That is why all that is taught about Aboriginal history in school is the theories of their migration.

But a history constituted of corroborated facts is not the only or indeed the most common way of dealing with one's past: it is rather the exception. In common with many other cultures, much of the substance of Aboriginal history is a number of very rich and varied myths narrated orally, and in other media such as song, dance, painting, naming, ritual and craft. To a European scholar, however, myths are merely 'fantastic stories', however powerful and meaningful are their metaphors and truths about the human condition. Simply because myths are not 'factual', they are discounted in European history. But because history is culturally produced, it must be structurally related to key features of the culture. It is no accident, therefore, that European history is thus constituted, for to value that form is to value change above stability, innovation above tradition and development above conservation. In other words, the very form of European history, quite apart from the massive partiality of its content, is part of a complex, powerful and highly culture specific value system which opposes any other. As dominant forms marginalise and de-legitimate other forms, the nature of European history thereby excludes Aboriginal.

So, along with the superficial appearance of the presentation of a common Australian substance to the history of the Australian people, these students also learn that school history is actually European history, that history is solely a matter of facts, and that the Aboriginal form of dealing with the past is not important. Because it was not this, nor I presume any other teacher's conscious intent to teach such matters to these students, such learning must be part of an implicit curriculum, and furthermore, an implicit curriculum which has not been generated by the individual teacher, but has been imposed on all teachers by the administration.

Because teachers' performance is often judged in relation to their ability to teach particular learnings, their critical incidents frequently reflect their difficulties in that regard. Reflecting back to teachers personally and privately, and collectively and publicly to the administration, the ways in which the problems teachers encounter are often produced by the unintended effects of what they are expected to teach, serves both to support teachers' professional judgement and assist the curriculum development process.

In that respect, this incident makes two important theoretical points: first, that because teaching is a cultural activity, values are inevitably taught; second, that because the curriculum is an enacted cultural structure, there will always be a number of overt and covert features supporting and reinforcing any particular values position. In this case, the analysis shows just how systematic, far-reaching and thorough values positions really are: they actively construct the curriculum. Such findings have clear and important consequences for educational administrators as much as for the teachers concerned. With regard to core curriculum, for instance, in a state like Western Australia where a centrally developed curriculum is fairly closely adhered to by the majority of teachers, such values must thus be reproduced throughout the state system. In a situation where individual teachers are responsible for developing their own syllabus and materials, although there will always be a hidden curriculum, there would be a far wider range of values transmitted through it. This incident should raise serious questions, therefore, about the advisability of core curricula. If teachers were in command of the kind of empirical evidence produced by the analysis of incidents such as this one, they might then be able to make a stronger contribution to such an issue, increasing their professional autonomy.

CONCLUSION

In these last three chapters I have tried to outline and illustrate some of the ways in which to analyse critical incidents. Many readers will find my account unsatisfactory because it is so general in some respects, and so much my own way of working with others. But in the end, analysis is a very personal affair. I find it is impossible to give an exhaustive account of what one does in analysing data, and I think it would be counter-productive in any case. In using data to inform professional judgement and action, one is more interested in the meanings one can produce and which one adopts rather than in constructing a single preferred meaning. That is to say, we should interrogate our conclusions, not in terms of the extent to which it is possible to get others to agree with us, but in terms of the questions, 'Why do I see it like that? How else could I see it?' and 'What do I consider the right way(s) of seeing it?'

Of course, when it comes to analysing critical incidents all approaches are much enhanced by getting other points of view. People tend to think that incidents should be analysed by the person who first describes them; but it is always useful, and often much easier, to include the ideas of others. The two most obvious possibilities here are the views of those with whom we can come into contact, and the views of others that we can read in published work. In the literature, the former category are generally known as 'critical friends' (Ingvarson 1986), and will include our colleagues, partners, tutors, advisers, superiors, and so on; and the latter category is mainly composed of research reports, though, of course, we take on ideas from many other sources in other media which we adapt in one way or another to our own situation.

I do not intend to elaborate on these sources of alternative analysis, as how who is invited to do what is a matter of personal preference, tolerance and negotiation. It is perhaps worthwhile just pointing out that the best analysis may come from those whom we do not usually invite to comment upon our professional practice, such as parents, and (dare I say it?) our students. But though it is necessary and useful to have our analyses evaluated and verified by others, as autonomous professional practitioners it is we who have to act upon and bear responsibility for our own perceptions of our practice. It is for this reason that I have, against my better judgement in some respects, gone as far as I have towards an algorithmic approach to the generation and analysis of critical incidents. It is most important that teachers are involved in all the phases and processes of classroom research, and to do that, they have to be able to do more than simply provide professional educational researchers with data for their projects. Simple step-by-step approaches are helpful initially, but they should be customised and relinquished as soon as possible.

So finally, and from my own experience again, the only way to learn to analyse critical incidents is to do it, and if the techniques I have outlined are one way of beginning to do it, then these chapters have served their main function.

Chapter 5

Developing a critical incident file

INTRODUCTION

Collections of phenomena and critical incidents have been around in one form or another for a very long time in every walk of life. Not only are biographies full of them, but every diary, collection of letters, log or journal tends to be built of critical incidents. Such records have an excellent pedigree as a valued strategy in many fields. Not only have they provided an essential data base for later researchers to examine, but in many branches of naturalistic research such as anthropology and ethnography, systematic collections of critical incidents in the form of journals are one of the very few universal and obligatory techniques. And in almost all branches of research, journals are used as adjuncts to other means of data recording and analysis. One not only finds them kept by other clinical and field workers such as zoologists, cartographers, archaeologists and sociologists, but also by physicists, mathematicians, linguists and medics.

But in spite of the ubiquity of this form of research instrument, their use has not been well recognised in professional development and educational research. And until recently there has been little in the literature on journal writing in education, and even less on critical incidents. In contrast, other forms of record keeping are well covered in the methodological literature. Yet, because critical incidents in teaching include a descriptive record, response and analysis upon which important judgements are made, they need to be constructed differently from merely anecdotal records. Also there probably need to be different kinds of critical incident appropriate to different fields of inquiry. Yet maybe there was more concern with the form in the past; C. Wright Mills, the great American sociologist, for instance, was a strong advocate of personal reflective records, which he called a 'research file' (1959) because it was organised thematically rather than chronologically.

It is partly his account of that idea and partly the need to escape the chronological associations of diaries, logs and journals that I have adopted the term 'critical incident file'. The teachers' professional record needs to be more than a log, for example, because the meaning and significance of what happened is more important to teachers than when it happened. This is also reflected in the term 'file', because it suggests it contains selected items important to a particular topic. Using the processes advocated here, the critical incident file can be a very effective way of developing the personal understandings of and theories about practice that informs all professional judgement.

THE CONSTRUCTION OF A PROFESSIONAL CRITICAL INCIDENT FILE

System

In Chapter 2 I suggested that one of the determining characteristics of critical incidents was the inclusion of essential detail; but perhaps a more important characteristic is that critical incidents are principally for the writer's own use: the aim is for the individual to use them to develop their own professional judgement in their own way and according to their own values. So, just as it is not possible to determine in general terms how much of what kind of detail is necessary in critical incidents, so it is not possible to lay down rules about what kind of system should be used to organise a critical incident file, or indeed how systematic it should be. Those considerations can only be decided by the purposes of the person who creates the file, and, also like the detail of the incidents, the system of a file should emerge as the incidents accumulate.

There are some general aspects that should be borne in mind, however. First, system is fundamental to all research, and if the progressive development of critical incidents occurs, then some kind of a system must be present, and will be reflected in form and content of the file. The point is that our system will determine not only what kind of incidents we include and which we analyse critically, but also other features which a critical incident file develops, such as how it becomes extended with regard to breadth and depth, for instance.

These extensions are quite straightforward, because they tend to be sequential: initially, a new concern is extended in breadth rather than depth, because of the way in which new issues arise. At first, before clear themes have emerged, it is not possible to distinguish the relevant from the irrelevant, the useful from the useless, the ideal from the practical, and so on, because these all depend upon our having some notion about what it is that we are seeking.

Most teachers' critical incident files begin with a wide-ranging exploratory phase, characteristic of which is the generation of a number of directions and beginnings. These may seem almost random at first, but they should not be seen as 'false starts' or 'wrong directions', because most are never developed. They are the essential range of possibilities and options, and we do not develop most of them for good reasons: they may be too peripheral, beyond the scope of action, or symptomatic of deeper issues. And sometimes we simply do not like them or we can later see better ways of approach. As demonstrated earlier, it is for such reasons that there is no such thing as a 'bad' critical incident file item: every item, however undeveloped, is the recording of something which then has the potential to be developed and used in other ways.

It is important to realise that the fact that many of the plethora of early items have not been further developed does not mean that it was unnecessary to think of them in the first place. It is highly unlikely for one to hit on the best or even a good direction immediately. Directions in understanding tend to change constantly, and it is only by generating a number of promising alternatives that one is likely to be found which is satisfactory in that it looks useful or interesting or likely to offer a solution to a problem being dealt with at that particular moment.

A wide range of ideas often appears at the beginning because a large backlog of observations and ideas which have been around in the mind of the teacher for some time are only now recorded, which tends to automatically extend the file in terms of breadth. After the burgeoning of the first few weeks it becomes necessary deliberately to extend the number of different ideas in a critical incident file to allow new ideas to emerge and new connections to be made. Breadth also ensures that the file continues to reflect the context of phenomena that are being pursued in depth.

Systematic extension in terms of depth can be achieved in a number of ways other than by turning more phenomena into critical incidents, though that is essential. One can also deepen a critical incident file through revision, re-analysis, further analysis, and categorisation and patterning of the phenomena. In practice, all these different operations tend to merge together, to suggest and entail each other. With regard to re-analysis, for instance, returning to re-read a record will not only suggest what further detail needs to be included, but it usually also generates other new items about the original entry. People often write, 'Did I really say that then? I've quite changed my mind about it, and now I think that...'. This is particularly true when phenomena are returned to for critique after some time. Examining and accounting for such shifts and revisions usually leads to deeper forms of analysis, re-analysis and meta-analysis, all of which are not really possible in the initial recording.

Re-reading earlier items tends to remind one of other related, subsequent instances and counter-instances. Following these not only leads to other kinds of analysis such as cross-referencing, but also leads to the recognition and development of patterns, trends and themes. All these are only possible when a number of items has accumulated. It is this reflection over time which narrows the content as later topics are selected for further development, making the items cohere and forcing us to categorise and pattern them. As such processes are performed on the individual items, so the whole critical incident file becomes more coherent and theoretical. It is these aspects of thinking and writing in depth which constitute the development of a systematic understanding which forms the knowledge base for understanding professional judgement.

As an instance of the way in which the existence of a phenomenon can be reflected on and then turned into a critical incident, the following is an item from an observer who was having some difficulty finding something to write about in her critical incident file. I had suggested that she record five minutes of a lesson where the teacher and students were talking to each other. It was a split-grade class of 9–11-year old remedial children. The observer was an adviser helping the teacher to use a language experience approach to literacy in which the children's learning was based on their own language. This transcription was part of what happened in the lesson:

Incident 24: Language experience

Teacher:	What shall we start with?
Student 1:	A capital letter. (*Laughter*)
Teacher:	Children! No! No!
Student 2:	A visit to the library.
Teacher:	Yes, we already know that's what it's about.
	(*Children remain silent*)
Teacher:	Well, we need to say when.
Student 3:	Thursday we went to the library.
Teacher:	What's another way of saying 'Thursday'?
Student 4:	Yesterday?
Teacher:	Yes. (*Writes on board*) Yesterday we went to the library.

At the time she wrote the phenomenon, she realised from her initial analysis that the tape recorder had revealed that what the teacher actually did was far from what she thought she was doing. Rather than using the children's own language, she was rejecting it by cueing them to produce hers. When the adviser showed the transcription to the teacher, their immediate response was a typical product of the practical problematic: how can I (you) change what you are doing to achieve better the aims in practice? At that point the phenomenon was merely a source of reflection in that the teacher realised she had still to shed some of her old habits.

It was only some weeks later when the adviser returned to re-read the phenomenon that she began to ask some very different and obviously critical questions which led into the broader social realm. These questions we formulated as: how it was that such a gap between the overtly stated intent of the teaching programmes and the teacher's implementation of them could occur? How it was that the inconsistency had not been noticed earlier? Why had teaching habits taken that particular form? How and why had they become habits in the first place? Such questions are clearly socially critical in that they demand social explanations and produce wider social meanings; but for various reasons she could not see or ask them initially. It was only because the account of the phenomenon was a record which made her initial perceptions available for reconsideration that, at a later stage, it was instrumental in something of a breakthrough in her perception of her work, and the social construction and situatedness of all teaching.

Audience

Another important feature of any writing is the intended audience; an author's perceptions of who will read their work, under what circumstances and for what reasons, must affect the writing in important ways. A critical incident file is written first and foremost for the use of the writer in the development of their professional judgement; but it is important for other reasons that a teacher's professional critical incident file facilitates the sharing of that knowledge with others. So although the major emphasis is that critical incident files must be personal documents for personal use, professional critical incident files cannot be purely private in the way that a diary may be. Some of a critical incident file should have a sufficient degree of 'publication' to make it intelligible to others. It is these sometimes conflicting requirements that make the issue of audience so important.

Thus, as is perhaps already clear, the principal attributes of 'mature' critical incidents are that they be precise and comprehensive. It is these features which make the critical incident file accessible to others. For this reason, publishers often distinguish between journals and notes, and the distinction is very important where the critical incident file, as a record of developing often random thoughts, is an important research tool.[1] Such 'notes towards an item' as, 'John hasn't finished his work again today', should not be edited out of the critical incident file, they should remain there so that the writer can develop them, if necessary into items which would make sense to an outsider with no access to the rest of the critical incident file. Ideally I think that a critical incident file should be written with at least three audiences in mind: primarily the writer him- or herself; second a critical friend such as a close colleague, facilitator or collaborating researcher; and third an interested (though not necessarily informed) public of other, individually unknown colleagues and researchers.

Because audience affects the language used, it is important to consider the language of the critical incident file in at least two ways: kinds and purposes of discourse. The two are of course, mutually constraining in that some things are best achieved or said in one kind of language rather than another. But in isolation, kinds of discourse can be considered most simply in the terms of the many writers, particularly Britton (1972), who have made us aware of the different kinds of language which we use, and how these different kinds of language are appropriate to different kinds of situations.

First, it is one of the major aims of the critical incident file to avoid the way in which the structure of essays and reports form a major constraint on the kinds of writing that are appropriate and hence, on the kind of thinking which is taking place. A critical incident file will include only a very few of the formal 'final draft' items because it should be a means of enabling the writer to think on paper. All items should originate as 'first drafts', which is a way of writing in which the purpose is to actually form thoughts through the process of writing. The purpose of the item is simply to hold something still on paper so that it can be further thought about.

Because so many teachers have been trained only to write final drafts for assessment by others after which they are seldom if ever read again by anyone, this kind of writing takes time and effort to develop. In trying to 'break set' with the essay form, some people go too far towards the diary form which tends to be first draft expressive writing with the writer as sole audience. Such is the following item:

Incident 25: Dear diary

To-day it rained, and I arrived at work soaked. It didn't make me in a very good mood exactly. I made the kids write and do worksheets most of the morning and read to them in the afternoon. When it was time to go, two parents came to see me about why their children weren't onto their own readers yet. Not a good day. I think I'm sickening for something.

There is little one can do with that as it is, except sympathise![2]

Language and purposes

Tying together these two key notions, namely, of a critical incident file offering a means for the development of ideas from an initial 'note for an item' to a well developed publishable (though still revisable) account, and the way in which the language of the critical incidents will change over that process, is Green's (1985) reconceptualisation of Britton's (1972) categories of transactional, expressive and poetic language. In Britton these three categories fulfil the functions of (a) getting things done, (b) expressing and exploring our perceptions, feelings and thoughts, and (c) crafting the language. He sees the transactional and poetic forms as growing out of undifferentiated expressive language. Green, however, shows how expressive language itself develops, not necessarily into the two other forms, but from private to public forms. This is an important concept with regard to professional critical incident file writing, because it accounts for changes in the language which cannot be dealt with in Britton's scheme. Most important of these changes is that the public form of expressive writing is language which aims to make available to others the feelings of the writer as an integral part of the information. That extra information is essential if an outsider is to read the item for meaning and significance within the context of the writer's experience. That is precisely the information that is written out of, for instance, transactional language. Knowing what it is that is being aimed for in the language of a professional critical incident file, is, of course, a great help in learning how to do it. What is being aimed at is simply precision and comprehensiveness in descriptions of phenomena, and generality in explanation of meanings in critical incidents.

Whilst traditional research writing is but one kind of transactional language in Britton's terms, it is important to be aware of some differences between theoretical and practical discourse within that genre, because these mark crucial differences in purpose. Most classroom discourse is of a practical nature: we talk about people, things, events, and relationships in highly specific situations. Theorisation and critique on the other hand, generally build towards generalisation and the inter-connection of a number of different instances.[3]

The danger here is that the language of critical incident files can be a cause of failure to meet the most basic research criteria. For instance, when a singular event is casually expressed in everyday life, we all too often say 'John does not' when we should actually say 'John did not', because, although in scientific terms it is seldom logical to generalise from only a few instances, in life we often have to make up our minds about something on the basis of a single instance. Similarly, we often say 'John does not' when we mean 'does not usually', for we ignore the 'John did' occasions because the 'John did not' are more frequent. It is, of course, a moot point in the philosophy of social science as to just what constitutes an adequate number of instances from which to generalise, but clearly frequency alone cannot constitute anything other than statistical significance.

However, given that we do not allow such matters to unduly inhibit action and judgement in our everyday lives, so also they should not prevent professional judgement in teaching, although our awareness of the problems should cause us to be rather sceptical and cautious. It is for that reason that I have stressed the effective use of these contrasting but complementary purposes of language.

The organisation of a critical incident file

In view of the necessity for continually adding to items, reviewing, linking and revising them, it goes without saying that any critical incident file is best kept on a word processor (or at least with separate items written on cards or loose-leaf paper). For this reason I do not favour strict chronological organisation of a critical incident file so that it looks like a journal, but find it much more appropriate to categorise items, keeping them in different files according to theme. That is, of course, the great advantage of keeping a critical incident file on a word processor: any item can be duplicated into any other file, or cross-referenced in such a way that items are indexed under different thematic categories, and they can be accessed through a simple 'sort' programme.

It is important to organise a critical incident file in such a way that it relates very directly to professional practice in order to facilitate ongoing theoretical thinking about it. As my practice is mainly writing and lecturing, I have mine organised according to lecture topics and potential papers. Amongst the categories I am currently using, are major topics such as 'observation', 'generalisation' and 'teachers' critical incidents', under each of which is a number of sub-files. Under 'teachers' critical incidents', for instance, at the moment there are eight sub-files, including 'implicit/curriculum', 'theory', 'values', and 'action research ideas'. Some of these such as 'theory' contain further sub-files: 'Piaget', 'theory-practice links', 'teachers' theory-in-use', 'teachers' espoused theories', and so on. Categories and files constantly change as new ideas become important, or I begin to accumulate enough on a topic to make a new file worthwhile; other topics are superseded when, for instance, I have finished a paper or have developed other interests. I also have a file of uncategorised items because I think it important to look at items a number of times over a period before classifying them, and even then I often reclassify them or duplicate them under several different headings. The outcome of this kind of thematic approach is demonstrated in the next chapter.

Developing a theme

As a final example, the idea of a professional critical incident file is well illustrated by an example of a series of seven incidents which have been thematically selected from over sixty made over a period of five months, the first being made towards the end of the first month. Notice how the particular theme is developed from writing about an overall concern: the matter of reading first appears to be just an extreme example of a general control problem. Overall the chronological record is well balanced between descriptions of what happened and what the teacher thought. So the final record provides a good historical account of her difficulties and steadily improving practice. It is a record which shows, quite typically, that the problem does not immediately materialise or manifest itself, but is progressively constructed as a result of the work she puts into observation and reflection.

Perhaps it is also interesting to note that she appears to be action researching her practice in the sense that she is deliberately finding out and hypothesizing upon what is happening, and then planning and monitoring change; she is clearly employing the action research spiral, and she does so through several distinct cycles. Also she is working at an essentially 'practical' level, recognising the constraints under which she works but not trying to change them, which would be a more 'critical' approach.

Finally, it is important to know that she is relatively inexperienced, and teaching a Year 4 class for the first time was having some difficulties with the different age group.

Incident 26: Reading 26 July

The day started on a happy note, but by lunchtime I was feeling frustrated with the behaviour in my class. They can't work for three quarters of an hour without me standing over them all the time. To add to my misery the Year 5 teacher added fuel to the fire!

'Goodness Jane, you certainly were airing your lungs again today! Even the children in my room were distracted by all the noise!'

I tried to explain my predicament and received little sympathy. 'Wait until they get to me. They'll soon have to shape up!' I felt an idiot. Obviously the noise had been troubling her for a long time and today was the final straw. The problem is definitely mine!

Even I am beginning to dread the time slot of 11 o'clock to 11.45. So full of interruptions and tension. Are three groups of ten so hard to manage? Isn't the reading set interesting enough? What is the children's attitude to reading?

Incident 27: Reading 28 July

Today was another showdown day with the school librarian. Eleven children hadn't returned their library books, the highest number ever. Another demerit point against Room D. The librarian really showed her feelings and told them that they were the worst class in the school, which was a reflection upon me.

Our 30 minutes library period had become another time filled with tension and fear related to reading. It's a real monster.

But what does the librarian do to promote reading, besides telling the children how bad they are? By the time the children have carded their own books they have barely 15 minutes to select books, and they are told to hurry along as there is another class coming soon. This period always leaves me feeling frustrated. The children don't have enough time to browse and choose their books. Do the children feel frustrated too? Could this be a reason why so many books are left at home and forgotten?

Shouldn't a librarian be teaching children more than carding their own books?

Incident 28: Reading 8 August

Today my suspicions were confirmed. I asked the children to rate four subjects, reading, maths, sport and spelling in order of their preference. Reading, for nearly half of the class was last. I had really expected maths or spelling, which I sometimes find tedious or boring.

At lunchtime I told the Year 4 and 5 teachers my findings. They agreed that the children's attitude to reading is poor according to my data, but tried to console me by saying that this attitude is quite normal for these children. Is it? It oughtn't to be. Surely my teaching method is at fault somewhere?

As I complained bitterly about the children's viewing habits, one fruitful idea was suggested. Why not use the television programmes that the children watch as a basis to get the children reading more? Great! Why hadn't I thought of this before?

Incident 29: Reading 24 August

The response to the TV celebrity board and celebrity scrapbook has been great. The children have been reading the newspapers and magazines to find out about their favourite TV characters or pop group.

Small group discussions have enabled them to communicate each other's findings, and I have noticed that they refer to the scrapbook frequently to back up their conversations.

Unfortunately just as I thought the situation was improving, the children's enthusiasm appears to be lagging. Could it be the end of term blues or has the novelty worn thin? Could the cause be timetabling constraints? Recently I haven't been allowing the children an opportunity to read to the class or discuss in their groups their findings. I really feel that by taking away the audience situation I have once again taken away their desire to read. The purpose of reading for others is important!

Incident 30: Reading 10 September

Just as I was beginning to feel as if I had at last captivated some interest in reading by creating a reading corner filled with lots of interesting books and all the comforts of home (e.g. beanbags and cushions) to create a cosy relaxed atmosphere, the children have taken the corner as an opportunity to devise mischief. I seem to be constantly reprimanding the children in the reading corner for the various antics they seem to get up to! Today was no exception. The noise level was mounting to a climax again. I boiled over with frustration. I had created another reading tension monster!

It's silent reading they cannot do! I'll now introduce time for silent, sustained reading daily to enable the children to experience this type of reading.

Incident 31: Reading 17 September

Today was our library period. What a pleasant surprise. Our new librarian didn't chastise any of the three children who didn't bring back their books on time, but gently reminded them that they should because other people would like to read them too. There was no tedious carding session. Instead the children were asked to sit quietly around her and to listen to a story called 'Crocodiles eat children'.

There was no wriggling or nudging, just eyes and ears captivated by the reader's skilled voice making the characters of the story come alive. My class were deeply involved, how tremendous! Naturally all the children wanted that book to read.

This session provided me with the one crucial link that was missing in my reading programme. I have encouraged the children to read, silently and aloud to each other and to me, but I did not often read to them a story simply to enjoy. I always had done this in the early grades I taught, but why not with these older children? These children need to be read to daily too; not necessarily a story, it could simply be a relevant topic of interest that arises within a day's work. I'm sure a read aloud session can still captivate these children's interest in reading.

Incident 32: Reading 27 September

The librarian had the children eating out of her hands again today. They lapped up every part of the story she was telling them. We both agreed that the children's attitude to reading has changed tremendously since she first encountered them, but I feel that she must take much of the credit for changing their attitude. She eliminated the dreaded demerit system and the dull carding of returned books. She doesn't hurry them in choosing their books, and is genuinely interested in the children's interests and extremely helpful in finding the right books for them. She has a memory like an elephant. Peter's never liked reading, but he's so pleased she kept a book on cars for him. This boosts his ego and he'll read it.

Lately I've found some of my children in the library at lunchtime. What are they looking for? 'You know...that book you read to us about...I want to read it!'

So I was right – it wasn't the children. Now they are finally beginning to look at reading as a pleasurable experience and at books as a source of delight.

CONCLUSION

The main point of this chapter has been that a teacher's critical incident file can and should contain all sorts of incidents at different stages of development towards the critical. Associated with this is the idea that it should be for more than just their private use. Continuing with this tension between writing a critical incident file for oneself and writing it for others, I think there are two main reasons for teachers to write for a wider public audience: one is that it is a way to educate the general public and university academics about the nature of their work; and the other is to enable them to network their ideas and experiences more effectively amongst each other. It is, of course, no accident that teachers are not expected or encouraged to share their expertise amongst themselves: whole sections of the profession have a vested interest in this not occurring.[4] Teachers lose to academics (like myself who gain professionally by collecting and publishing teachers' experiences), to employers (who can control the direction of change in schools), to consultants (who are paid as a conduit of teachers' ideas).

Case conferences are becoming increasingly common in even the most traditional schools, and it is not difficult to imagine a similar period each week in which teachers are given the time to discuss the phenomena they have observed, collectively rendering them critical. This is, after all, what I do in my courses, though with teachers from different schools. We spend anything from half an hour to three hours discussing the content of our files.

Such sessions can occur far more easily in schools that are actively seeking change; indeed, it facilitates change. The creation of critical incidents can help to overcome the tensions between individual teachers and whole school change. On the one hand, we now know that the unit for effective and lasting change is the structures of the whole school; on the other, we know that it is teachers who change schools by changing themselves. Whole schools change their administrate structures, teachers change teaching and learning. Schools change only when each guides and facilitates the other. Thus whole school approaches have to engage teachers at a personal level.

One way of helping an individual teacher to generate an agenda for personal change within the context of the aims for the whole school, and to suggest structural changes necessary to facilitate teaching changes, is to work on connecting the specifics of their teaching and learning practice to wider issues through critical incidents. For example, Incident 12: *Manners* and Incident 24: *Language experience* relate to these different aspects of change, one to how whole school structures manifest themselves in the classroom, the other to how classroom events may require system level approaches. Others such as Incident 13: *Air pressure* show how concerns are focused on teaching and learning. There is no reason why critical incidents should not be shared and collected, both to facilitate the change and to record the progress of the change process to share directly with other schools, eventually becoming a common technique in school improvement.

Chapter 6

An example of a critical incident file

INTRODUCTION

The main aim of this chapter is to consolidate some of the points made thus far by presenting further examples of teachers' critical incidents in the form of a thematic file. The secondary aim is to illustrate some typical everyday concerns of practising teachers. Many of the examples of critical incidents included in this chapter and book are, of course, not really mine, having been written by the teachers I work with. Because the actual incidents are given as they were written (in the raw, so to speak), they reflect various stages of description and analysis. Many of the incidents are truly embryonic in that the observer recognises that there may be something to say, but is not yet sure quite what, and so has just described a phenomenon (an incident, comment or feeling) and asked some initial questions. As suggested earlier, these are not really critical incidents because nothing is explained and no wider meanings have been drawn; but they are included to show the kind of development in skill and understanding which can take place as one becomes more familiar with the form.

In the previous chapter I mentioned the value of organising instances as a file as entries begin to accumulate rather than as a journal. Here I shall illustrate this by showing how I constructed themes about teachers' critical incidents from reading a number of them. First, I deliberately set out to look for some themes. Because a critical incident file should always contain reflections upon the general themes of the incidents in it, I include my account of this process here. I began with the following observation:

Incident 33: Categories of critical incident

The people in this group seem to be presenting incidents in an almost thematic way. It seems so obvious that I don't think I am just imposing it, so perhaps it's coming from the interactions within the group as they share and analyse their experiences. They seem to proceed in a series of, 'Yes, but... (example)', 'Yes, and... (example)', 'Yes, if... (example)', 'Yes, when... (example)', 'Yes, because... (example)', and so on, so it would be surprising if themes did not emerge. But overall they seem to provide more examples about three major themes. These could be called, 'When the student(s) caused the teacher a problem', 'When the teacher caused the student(s) a problem', and 'Isn't this interesting?' Over half the entries discussed this week concerned some kind of misunderstanding.

I used those categories of event as some of the themes in which to organise this file. This involved some change to the incidents I wanted to use because I had originally analysed them from the point of view of their usefulness to teachers who were writing critical incidents as a means of informing themselves about their teaching so that they could improve it. Constructing this file in order to show others how to do it, meant that I had to become more evaluative of the form and the content of the incidents, and what the original writers had done with them. In that regard, many of the incidents presented here are good examples of the fact that purpose determines the analysis, and thus that re-analysis is often required for a different purpose.

This should correct any impression readers may have that I performed these analyses instantly: some of these examples have been re-worked up to five years later. That can be a virtue rather than a vice: all analysis of any kind of data is in a deep sense provisional, but whereas in other kinds of research an analysis tends to be taken as final if it has been well done, critical incident analysis is explicitly temporary, and should capitalise on the ease and value of subsequent re-analysis, both to provide a deeper understanding and to analyse different aspects in different ways for different purposes.

This explains why, even when important things do very obviously stand out in an incident, quite different and equally important ideas may occur later as we re-examine the incidents with different concerns in mind. Three good examples of such re-worked entries are Incident 7: *Finishing work*, Incident 21: *Waste*, Incident 46: *Lock-step thinking*. I think it important that such long-term re-working should not be a luxury afforded only to academics, however. Time to periodically take stock, revise and consolidate ideas and positions, should also be available to teachers, because they have to act upon their professional judgement which derives from an understanding of themselves and their teaching. Reference to and a re-reading of a critical incident file is most helpful in that process.

In that regard, there may be some confusion here about what I am doing and why. In one sense the reader should not be misled by the number of teachers' critical incidents into thinking that I am directly portraying a teacher's critical incident file in this section. I am teaching an in-service course, and the extracts are from my critical incident file. Because I have so little direct contact with them, much of my reflection on my teaching is reflection upon what the teachers have written for the course. But because I am reflecting in the main on how they are developing professionally, much of my analysis is critical in the sense that I am looking for points at which understanding and growth could occur. The critical incidents are therefore me as an academic reflecting upon the learning and development of my students, and so what is primarily on display is a teacher-educator's critical incident file, in spite of the fact that many of the incidents are teachers' accounts of their practice. There are relatively few entries like the one above which are mine alone.

With regard to audience, I have shifted in the presentation from using the file to work out ideas for myself to presenting ideas from the file for others. To do this I have had to write short explanatory passages that link the selected incidents together to develop the theme coherently. None of this 'thematic bridging' was written in the original file. But without it readers would merely be presented with a catalogue of incidents. That is one useful way to present a file for some purposes, but when one is trying to communicate a theme, the incidents are used to illustrate points made in the discussion of the themes. Critical incidents can always be looked at in a number of different ways, so it is necessary to explain what one is seeing in them. Because it is necessary to articulate the incidents, it is quite possible, as I do here, for one person to produce a public document that contains incidents written by others.

A CRITICAL INCIDENT FILE

Theme 1: Embryonic entries

Feelings only   This first incident is a good example of where most teachers start in their analysis. Like most initial attempts, this one is very easy to improve.

Incident 34: Geometrical theorems

Friday: Period 7 and 8 – Proof of Geometrical Theorems. The attempts to fill in the sheets had not been good and the lesson was very 'flat' going through them. Some of the brighter ones seemed to understand, but others just found it hard going.

This has all the hallmarks of under-developed description: impressionistic judgements, lack of precision, and an absence of any concrete examples. For instance, 'Some of the brighter ones seem to understand, but others just found it hard going' is language appropriate to recording impressions, but is not very precise. What is meant by 'seemed' and 'understanding', and why 'some'? A good test of an account of an incident is whether it is possible to generate specific hypotheses about it from the data it contains. It is not possible to answer any general questions (such as 'Am I teaching well?' which are themselves extremely vague and beg all kinds of other questions) let alone any specific questions such as 'What did which students find "hard going" about which theorems?'

Improvement of the description of the incident, however, is not the only way to improve this account, because there is no such thing as pure description in any case: any description is but a selection of data, thought and experience, so reflection on and analysis of how and why this occurred in this instance, should appear somewhere. At some stage, though not necessarily when first written, some indication as to why this was chosen as an entry and how it was problematic to the writer should be added. The point, however, is that even as it is quoted this is not a 'bad' entry, but merely an embryonic one which at present just records the teacher's sense of unease. Because so much teaching is actually the management of personal relations, it is very important to record our feelings; but the entry needs further development if it is going to do anything else as well, such as explain what was causing those feelings.

Thought only   Here is another embryonic incident of a different kind. In my professional practice I work more with ideas than with people and events in the material world, so my entries are more often accounts of what I have been thinking about than of what I have been doing. Consider the following:

Incident 35: Piaget

I do not believe that children really see the world as Piaget suggests. He's made the basic assumption that *a priori* logical reasoning is the highest form of human behaviour and achievement. That's a value and it affects the development of his theory. Having espoused the idea, he was bound to see adults as being better at the higher forms of reasoning than children because he could hardly then have held that children, with their bizarre ideas and nonsensical answers to his questions, were operating with the same processes at the same level as adults.

As it stands, there is nothing concrete in this entry. It is really just an account of a conclusion which needs some concrete 'for instance...' as supportive evidence, even if it is only the citation of an example from Piaget's work, to validate it. Without this, one can only note the comment, one cannot even effectively challenge it because the reader does not know exactly what it was a conclusion about.

Action only   The next entry demonstrates the opposite omission: it is all concrete facts; there is no thought or feeling:

Incident 36: Spontaneous planning

English first, today, followed by Maths. We discussed the *Space* article, and then began on area. They got the idea of counting tiles quickly, and finished too early. I was just wondering what to do when I saw Sam measuring the top of his desk. So for the last ten minutes we all measured things and calculated the area. We started a list of what was what on the board. Had an extended lunch hour because the superintendent came late to talk to us.

Here we have only a narration of what happened, a kind of blow by blow account, but no reflection or generalisation of any kind. So there are dangers in recording only feeling or thought or action when more than a single aspect is necessary to understand the issue being concentrated upon. As they stand, these three incidents are little more than factual log-like entries. But they should not be excluded from the file on those grounds, because it is important to record what we thought worth reporting, and because once recorded it can be thought about at some other time. Furthermore, it is not always possible to think about one entry in isolation: it is only when we have a series of events to consider that we can begin to understand what is happening and are able to write a 'thoughtful' entry from a reading of several predominantly thought, feeling or action entries. So the point is that all three aspects should be included, and constant re-reading and revision may be necessary to do it.

Theme 2: Common incidents

Student misunderstandings and/or errors   As I recorded in Incident 33: *Categories of critical incident* above, in my experience by far the most common concern of teachers is how and why students misunderstand them, particularly their instructions and the tasks they set. It is only by recording and closely examining students' misunderstandings, that teachers can use them as growth points for all concerned. The professional critical incident file is a good way to do that. As an example, the following is a typical early entry of that kind:

Incident 37: Ben's problem

Day 6. Today I discovered something quite alarming. Ben, the bright spark in the class, could not work out a fairly straightforward problem in a maths test: 'There were 18 chairs to be shared amongst 9 boys. How many did they have each?' He had several attempts at the answer but each time he became more confused himself. I think it was a blow to his ego because he rarely makes a mistake. It was compounded by the fact that he knew other children were having no trouble with the question. I think the reason he had trouble with it was that he couldn't picture the problem as a real situation. More exposure to this type of thing will probably help.

Although this teacher is on a useful track in her concern with the student and the problem, she does not yet appear to know quite how to develop that concern in terms of either analysis or action. With regard to the necessary diagnosis prior to action, this is a potentially interesting entry which is neutralised by a notable lack of data. There is no indication that anyone tried to discover from the boy whether it really was 'a blow to his ego' or not, or even whether the assumption that he could not picture the problem was the root of his difficulty, though it's a very insightful hypothesis.[1] Uninvestigated hypotheses about motive or cause are always dangerous, but they are doubly so when they are not formulated from data in a way that allows for some kind of verification process, even if no attempt at verification is made then.

One kind of data that would help here would be the history of the problem: had the child been taught division as 'division' or 'sharing', for instance. Another would be to get Ben's reaction to the teacher's hypothesis. It also always helps to generate a number of alternative hypotheses upon which different action could be reasonably planned. With regard to helping this teacher with the immediate problem, the lack of data makes such an entry extremely difficult for an outsider to comment upon validly. There may have been something in the context of the question (which we do not know), some other ambiguity which only the brightest child would perceive and thus have difficulty with. Without even such a simple and easily accessible form of data as the test format being presented to the reader, one has to fall back on mere speculation.

However, it is only if an initial record is made that such problems can become apparent: the entries can always be developed and many of the gaps filled in later. Unless one starts somewhere, one has nothing to work on. However limited this entry was in terms of data for analysis, it did nevertheless clearly indicate to this teacher a feature of her practice needing understanding. What it revealed was that she was about to give the boy more of the same. Once she could see that as a typical 'autopilot' routine, she decided to try something quite different. So seldom if ever are any entries a total waste – there is almost always something to engage. Although this was a not a very useful incident as it stood, it was an excellent starting point for developing both a more appropriate entry and an understanding of professional critical incident writing.

Although the next incident similarly needs more data and analysis from the students' viewpoint, the fuller account provided is a much better basis for critique of a routine because there is more scope for alternative hypothesis formation, and alternative hypotheses can challenge our existing perceptions of a situation.

Incident 38: History exam

I have been marking some Year 9 History examination papers. I am amazed at some of the problems some of the students had and some of the mistakes that were made. The examination paper had clear instructions on the front page to write the answer to sections A and B on the examination paper. The answers to Section C (essays) were to be done on the separate sheets of paper provided.

Seventy-five students sat for this examination. Eight students answered sections A and B on the separate sheets of paper. Four students answered section C on the examination paper – with much difficulty. However, the biggest problem, from my position as marker, was that twelve students forgot to put their names on their examination papers. These errors are amazing. The students know to read the instructions and most of them should know their own name (!!???!). I am unable to understand how these mistakes could occur – especially amongst 14-year-olds.

The main problem that the students had was not reading the question properly or not answering the question that was asked. In the first instance, where the question asked 'give three of something' many students gave two, four or even six, in one case. Inexplicable! In the second instance, where the question asked 'who did something?' many students either put down the date or the country where it occurred. Astounding!

As far as I can tell, so far, the majority of students are rushing into and through their examinations. They are not taking time to read what should be done and what should be answered. The importance of reading the instructions and the questions has been emphasised time and time again. Yet still the students do not do this. I do not know how this can be overcome, except by continuing to emphasise the importance of this reading and hope that one day it sinks into the student's total awareness of the situation.

We all tend to blame others before we blame ourselves, so another commonly unquestioned routine is the tendency to blame students when they do something wrong. Unfortunately, it is all too easy to construe teaching/learning difficulties in terms of the inadequacies of the students, because they seldom have the opportunity to respond. The trigger for my alternative hypothesis in this entry was that the teacher confessed that he was unable to understand the mistakes the students made when they 'know how to read the instructions'. Clearly, although they may know how to read the instructions, they are not actually doing so, or at least not doing so with retention and understanding. So the question we should really ask is, 'What can have interfered with the learning of this apparently obvious procedure?' That question, significantly, is not the one posed by this teacher, and hence reveals a feature that might repay investigation.

Again, we can only hypothesise, but generating a specific hypothesis provides something to check out, some further engagement with the problem for this teacher. My hypothesis, derived incidentally from observation of my own teaching, was that when this teacher gave a paper to the students with instructions written on it, habitually he would then stand at the front of the class and both read and explain the instructions orally. Whereas we might think that we are thus teaching the children to read the instructions, through the more powerful implicit curriculum we are more likely to be teaching the children that there is no need to read the instructions for themselves because the teacher will read and explain them (in all their boring detail) orally. An examination would be the first situation of the year where this would not occur, hence the number of mistakes made because students had never actually been asked to read the instructions for and by themselves.

Once such a hypothesis has been generated, it is then possible to observe one's habitual practice to check it out and form others. I emphasise the necessity for such hypotheses, because otherwise most of us simply fall to blaming the students, and attempt to rectify the problem by giving them more of the same. Contrary to an impression given by some research reports, hypotheses do not have to be 'correct' to be useful. This teacher may be 'right' in that it is simply a matter of his students rushing the questions, but that does not mean the alternative hypothesis is 'wasted'. Oral introductions may be a feature of this teacher's practice while not causing the particular problem of this incident. So it may also be something to attend to for other reasons on another occasion. Such 'wrong' hypotheses thus accumulate as a repertoire of possibilities for other cases and situations. They constitute a kind of stock of working knowledge or professional wisdom, and as such must contribute towards improved judgement. Overall, hypothesis formation and subsequent 'clinical' investigation is a relatively secure and unthreatening means of beginning to work on the values implicit in a routine. And if investigations are honestly conducted they always pose more questions than they answer.

Incident 39: Volume formula

I assumed some knowledge of volume – we have used unit cubes to find volumes a couple of months ago – and on the blackboard we went over the methods for finding the volumes of prisms with some numerical examples. We then found the relationship between the volume of a cuboid and the volume of a pyramid using water and pouring from a cuboid. It appeared that everyone had understood, but as the students were copying down the examples I found one girl asking another what the difference between volume and surface area was. I was shocked. I talked to her and she appeared to understand at the end of the discussion. I had assumed that they could retain the concept of volume from a previous lesson some time ago, but I should have used a more concrete method even for these advanced students.

Here is another example of an early entry which needs further analysis and some hypothesis generated. It is indeed surprising to find any able 14-year-old mathematics student who apparently does not know the difference between volume and surface area. Because it is surprising, it should not be taken at face value: any counter-instance of these students' generally good grasp of mathematical concepts needs to be accounted for in some way. One diagnosis might be that she had forgotten that surface area is 'side × side', but volume is 'side × side × side'. Perhaps she was actually merely asking the difference between the two formulae, because she had forgotten the structure of the formal operation involved. Another possibility is that she was using the surface area formula for volume by mistake, and realising that the two were thus the same, would ask how the two should differ, because she knows they must be different. It is interesting that this teacher's response was to talk her into an understanding, rather than to diagnose the cause of the confusion. The substitution of further teaching for diagnosis is, of course, another occupational hazard in a transmission approach to teaching. Even as it stands, if we ask the critical question, 'What is this an instance of?', and we see that it is an example of a student attempting to resolve a mathematical problem by simply remembering a formula, we have revealed a great deal about the student's view of how to do maths, a matter of immediate practical concern to the teacher.

I have spent some time on these last four examples because I have found that teacher's write more critical incidents about students' misunderstandings than any other single category. Of course, it is not possible to explicate every instance, but it is very possible and necessary to use the instances to generate specific hypotheses which can then be checked out. Students do misunderstand, but it is seldom because they cannot understand: most often it is because they understand something else. The fact that they are so often left with the misunderstanding actually tells us something important about teacher–student relationships.

Problems teachers cause students The second common kind of incident teachers often observe concerns problems they cause their students. This is another common category because most teachers are so concerned about it, though it is often very difficult to recognise such instances.

Incident 40: Clinton and James

When two 'live wires' team up as friends, my job becomes doubly difficult. Clinton and James are two such 'live wires' and whenever together, are constantly talking. This morning everyone was on the floor reading aloud their creative writing. Clinton and James were told to stop talking, once – twice, then I separated them. A short while later, the two were separated again, with Clinton being given a permanent place at my feet. The boys were told not to sit near each other ever again.

On the way over to the television room the children walk in lines with a specific partner. Half-way across the yard, I noticed Clinton and James together at the end of the line, while Shane, James' partner, was second apart. The group walked on to the television room, where they were to watch a film with three other classes. Clinton and James were not allowed to watch the film and spent the time picking up papers with a couple of other children and a teacher.

Incident 41: A lesson from the children

The disruptive nature of the combination of Clinton and James has been discussed in previous journal entries. However, I learnt a lesson today. The class had been told to come and sit on the floor, and I was going to read something to them about Australia. Since it took a long time for everyone to complete their tasks and sit on the floor, I was beginning to get very short-tempered. 'Whoever isn't seated by three will not get a point', I threatened. At this the pace quickened and finally everyone was on the floor. The lesson began. Suddenly I realised that Clinton, who had been given express orders to sit at my feet on all occasions, was near the back of the group, and that James was up the front. I glared at Clinton and said, 'What are you doing there? You should be here, where I can keep my eyes on you!' Clinton replied, 'But James is sitting there and I aren't allowed to sit near him.'

Comments It was interesting to see the logic behind Clinton's excuse. True, James had come to join the group on the floor before Clinton and so Clinton reasoned that his best move would be to sit as far away from James as possible. My immediate reactions had been too hasty – because I saw the situation in terms of one of disobedience and/or that Clinton and James had forgotten what the rules were. I was shown that I need to be less hasty in my reactions and actions.

This is a good example as it links together separate incidents which occurred at different times, but which are contingent. The teacher's comments are not so much an analysis as an admission, and as such fairly negative. Instead of leaving it there, the kind of questions that could be asked are, 'How often do such situations occur? How may they be recognised?' and, 'How can they be avoided?'

As is sometimes the case, however, it is possible to explicate such situations by recourse to theories found in the literature. In this case Gregory Bateson's *Steps Towards an Ecology of Mind* is useful, because he examines the stresses placed on an individual's psyche by what he terms a double bind, which is more commonly known as a 'Catch 22' situation. Students are often put in a position in which they can only do one thing or another, and whatever they do is wrong by different rules. This can occasionally occur accidentally, as in this case, but it can also occur intentionally when, for instance, it is used as a means of discipline. For instance, I can remember, as a student myself being asked why I had done something, and then when I began to give what I considered to be the relevant reasons, being told I would be punished for making excuses for my behaviour. Exploring situations like this, which are common to a number of quite different social situations, tends to lead to a personal awareness of the possibility that such situations do occur, and hence to a more efficient avoidance of them.

Such problems as double binds are very difficult to act upon, but that does not put them outside the scope of a teacher's professional judgement: such incidents are an important part of understanding our practices, and can often lead to radical changes in understanding and awareness. I believe that changing the way we solve our practical dilemmas and our preferred responses does achieve real curriculum change; but because they may be no more than subtle shifts in how we see ourselves and our relations to others, they tend to pass unnoticed and unacknowledged. Using critical incidents is one very effective means of recognising implicit changes and thus (by making them explicit) of attaching appropriate importance to them. One has to have a high degree of confidence to take responsibility for things that do not go right, so it is indicative of teachers' professionalism that such items are common amongst teachers' critical incidents. Unfortunately, in most schools teachers do not usually discuss such things with their colleagues: the prevailing ethos is that one does not make mistakes rather than that one shares them with colleagues, so all may support each other and learn from them.

I encourage teachers to use action research to turn such concerns (which are generally little more than vague intuitions) into assured and responsible teaching practices. In the following entry, for example, the teacher posed an important question but needed help in dealing with it.

Incident 42: Craft lesson with surprise visit

The theme on trees and plants is going very well and the children seem to be enjoying the lessons and associated craft activities. The craft lesson today was on mural buildings, but more specifically on making people from another planet. The children had discussed, this morning, what people on 'The Planet of the Mushrooms' would look like and the characteristics were listed on the board, with a model of the actual 'beings' being created on the board, too. Each part of the model had been made. I had drawn around the head and stalk and eyes and the children were to cut them out. As a class we went through the steps for making the arms, legs and mouth. Despite the explicit step by step instructions given, the children were constantly asking me how to do steps l, 2, 3 etc. They were all working at different rates. I felt like screaming. 'Watch me again', I yelled. Hello Mrs L.! (Special Education Advisory Teacher). Her surprise visit threw me into confusion. The children were excited and wanted to show her what they were doing – legs were on backwards, eyes coloured green, mouths all different! I felt embarrassed that the children hadn't done the work properly, although I know Mrs L. well, and she knows the children. Being a perfectionist, I want good work. Both Mrs L. and I know the children's limited ability but I still feel threatened by it.

Comment. Why did the children have so much trouble pasting on the mouth? On the other hand, I must really review my perfectionist nature and high ideal expectations and think in terms of the real level of ability of the class.

The phenomenon in this case is students being asked to do something beyond their capability. This class was a remedial withdrawal group, and the teacher, by pre-determining a particular outcome, had turned what was ostensibly a manual craft lesson into a mental comprehension lesson. Apart from cutting and pasting there was in fact very little 'craft' involved, certainly there was no 'design', which is a key characteristic of craft as opposed to mere labour. Instead there was an enormous amount of comprehension of highly specific instructions: the children had to follow a particular sequence of actions, and operate according to a very precise spatial requirement.

The entry also shows how an incident (in this case the way in which the teacher felt embarrassed in front of an outsider) can indicate issues which turn out to be quite different from the practical problematic of, in this instance, how to get the children to make mushroom people correctly. This was an entry made after nine weeks' practice in critical incident writing, and the change that has occurred as it so often does, is that the teacher was quite prepared to acknowledge and consider the practical implications of her personality traits and values for her teaching. That is a very risky business. Recognising that she had a particular trait enabled her to bring it out into the open, and once she had done that she was then able to work upon it.

Working upon it does, of course, not necessarily mean changing it: it may involve looking for other less frustrating ways of demanding a high standard, which would not have detrimental effects upon 'craft' lessons in terms of freedom for the children to create according to their own ideas. The fact that this teacher did not see immediately that she had adopted what I thought was an inappropriately designed craft lesson for these low-ability children, and that she did not see the appropriateness of the students all working at different rates, is not of great consequence here, although both offer excellent possibilities for change. The main purpose of such incidents is to provide a way to understand aspects of teaching/learning, and this one is effectively used in that way. The point this teacher raised for herself and about herself provided plenty to work upon; that others can see more and different things shows that there is an oversupply of possibilities. One must be careful not to try to raise and deal with everything at once, as that is discouraging and confusing. Some incidents which touch upon the feeling that aspects of teaching are creating problems for students and can be improved, reveal very deep and potentially disabling fears about teaching skills. The following appears to be such an entry:

Incident 43: What's History?

Today's lesson was one of revision for the examinations which commence tomorrow, for Year 8s. The students were to use the time for study and asking any questions on sections of the course that they might not understand – not what is actually asked in the examination. For today's entry, I would like to relate one question and answer episode with one student.

'Sir, Sir!' called Andrew, wagging his arm in the air.

'Yes, Andrew', I replied.

'Why do we have to know all these things in History?' he asked.

'What things do you mean?'

'All these facts about other people who have lived so long ago: it doesn't really matter what they did does it? It has nothing to do with us.'

'Well', I began, 'History is more than facts. I told you at the beginning of the year that facts and dates are really not the important parts of learning History. In History, it is more important to know why people have done something, why they have behaved or reacted in a certain way. This is the way we can understand how and why we are here today.'

'But I don't really care about why people have done things in the past', replied Andrew.

'But you will care as you learn more and more about what has happened. The older you become the better you will be able to relate to and understand the effect man's past has had on the direction of his progress.'

'I suppose...' was the final comment.

At this stage I was diverted to answering other pressing questions from other students. I doubt if I really convinced Andrew, but it did remind me how difficult it can be to explain this type of concept to a 13-year old.

This is again a fairly typical entry for an early stage of critical incident writing, which shows a subtle adherence to the practical problematic and an autopilot routine. The teacher's overtly stated concern about this exchange was that the student had not really accepted that 'history is more than facts'. As a history graduate, the teacher knows that history is in a real sense more than facts, so as the student does not share his view, he assumes that his explanation or the student's cognitive ability may have been inadequate. But the reality this teacher ignores or suppresses, is that for whatever reason his students do actually see history as being 'facts about other people', and the past merely as the past. The teacher's response denies the learner's view of his teaching, and significantly (thankfully?) he is then diverted from the issue by 'other pressing questions'. Could anything be more pressing than critiquing a teaching of history which does not concern historiography, only its outcomes; does not introduce students to people, but to facts about them; and which does not enable students to see the presence of the past, only its pastness?

Such an entry makes the necessity for a critical friend (mentor? therapist?) clear. All writing expresses and disguises dispositions, particularly values. Sometimes what a writer writes says more about the writer than about the phenomenon they write about. Breaking down assumptions in order to proceed with research prior to planning changes to practice is a process which requires a very gentle and reassuring touch from an other person, and a great deal of courage from the teacher.

As we saw in the previous example, it may happen that people record a phenomenon for a reason of which they are consciously aware, but when they come to re-read and examine it, they find there are other much deeper and more subtle reasons for having selected it, of which they were unaware at the time. In the above case, what appeared at first to be a straightforward practical phenomenon actually turned out to be a subtle theoretical problem which went right to the root of this teacher's practice. Unless the teacher had described the incident, the subtleties would never have been available for further analysis and explication, and unless I (in a tutor-as-facilitator role) had offered an alternative (far more frightening) reading, this teacher would have been quite happy to regard the matter as a common but minor failing in communication or conceptualisation, thereby failing to confront the problem of how it is that his teaching as a whole not only failed to communicate the true nature of history to this student and no doubt others too, but also communicated a misunderstanding about the nature of the discipline and his view of it.

Transcripts are a very important source of phenomena. In contrast to the traditional research requirements that the transcript be taken from an actual recording of the incident, for a critical analysis of one's own teaching, a written account of how we have remembered what happened is often far more useful because our account is our reconstruction of the event, and so can also reveal how we thought about it.

Theme 3: Personal style

Perhaps the best way to conclude this chapter is to hand the account back to two practising teachers both of whom demonstrate in quite different ways different kinds of awareness of self and practice. In these entries the writers are relating their practice to who they are and questioning their roles as teachers. The first teacher has a style of writing which (bearing in mind questions of audience and purpose) is perfectly suited to both a public account and informing individual practice.

Incident 44: Private territory

Sometimes a school seems like an archdiocese: each classroom represents a parish – occasionally there is a visitation, but mostly our attempts to save souls – our success and failure – remains our own affair and goes unnoticed. Until some evangelist appears in the guise of a superintendent, replete with some new interpretation of some holy text (viz. the gospel according to James Britton), we stumble along our own road to Emmaus.

Well, today Mrs P lavished praise on my class. Most teachers (from experience and observation) have a highly developed proprietorial sense about their classes and the space they occupy. This seems to be bound up with self-esteem as much as anything. There is a sense too in which each individual teacher is a performer who knows his or her audience. The relationship is often very subtle; no amount of quantitative research will expose the fragile and delicate tracery of that relationship. Even to introduce a third party – however self-effacing, tactful and sensitive – is to diminish the effectiveness of that 'performance'.

These comments imply, I suppose a certain role for the teacher – certainly not the teacher as facilitator. But now that I've written that, I realise it's wrong, it's not what I meant to write at all. I've oversimplified something fairly nebulous, something fluid, something provisional. Yes. There is a measure of dramatic performance, but it does not exclude the teacher assuming a more diffident role either. I didn't mean to argue a case against granting passports to outsiders, nor to introducing a measure of self-examination and reflection; I just wanted to establish my view of the teacher as a rather lonely, isolated practitioner, fairly jealous of his or her territory.

Back to Mrs P. Does what we do in the privacy of our classrooms inspire our colleagues? I'm trying here to get beyond the obvious: We know the opposite, the teacher whose class riots for 40 minutes and then comes to you for a poetry lesson. The class that is! But our basic philosophy as indicated through our teaching styles, choice of materials, class-room regime and our expectations – those things that we value, do they affect colleagues? Students? Students have to cope with these differences, adjust, come to terms with them during a working day. Here's an example.

Example: A matter of presentation   I have a Year 10 student named Vic. He is a bright lad and we get on very well. Curiously enough the other day he was writing an essay about student attitudes towards 'work'. I must add that it was not a very sophisticated or thorough analysis but it was candid and astute. One of the observations he made was to point out that students learned what the teacher wanted and they then gave it back to them – not in terms of assignments and essays and such like, but in terms of presentation and treatment.

Now, in spite of what you might think – and if I were in your shoes I would be sceptical – Vic arrived at this conclusion by himself. It was obvious enough to him. He was conscious of its effect on the quality of work (that is, in terms of real learning) a student might produce: he even went so far as to suggest that such behaviour implied a particular view of what schooling was all about. He then went off to Social Studies.

A few minutes later I had to go to the office and I passed the Social Studies room. There was Mrs P. on her knees examining an enormously long scroll. I went into the room to have a look too. It was a project on India. Beautifully presented: drawings, charts, diagrams, maps and typewritten sheets. The layout too was excellent. Mrs P. and I chatted for a while. Yes. It was Vic's work. Just finished. Took him two weeks. Well, perhaps it was unfair but I asked him some questions on what he had done.

At first I was genuinely interested and wanted to know certain things. But it dawned on me that Vic had suddenly seen something else in these questions – an attempt by me to remind him of his own ideas concerning students and work, and the irony of his present situation: praised and applauded for a project which was basically a performance. This seems so deeply ingrained – the production of an artefact; the concentration upon the end product – as to be virtually ineradicable. But there seems to be an association in the student's mind between such artefacts and what's valuable. It doesn't matter how it is achieved or produced, but it and it alone has supreme value. What I value and promote (or so I believe) is process, which is perhaps far harder to grasp – at least for a student.

Do they just serve each teacher according to his or her expectations? Do they see the inherent contradictions? Do they satisfy teacher A while, in truth, valuing teacher B's approach more highly? And why is it valued? Are certain teachers more persuasive? Is it something to do with parent/student expectations reflecting those of a larger community? How does the student see his or her own role and relationships with others, particularly the teacher? How did I get here when I began where I did?

This seems to me to be well-written for others as well as for the writer himself. He is a writer who thinks on paper very effectively and also obviously enjoys it. It is not everyone who can write like this, nor is it a style which I personally would attempt; but it is a style, and anything that is written with style usually makes good reading. Structural changes have occurred: the three incidents (Mrs P. praising his class, Vic's ideas about product, and Vic's project) are not just narrated, but are thematically linked; other thoughts, experiences and hypotheses have been introduced to analyse the incidents and explain the perceived themes. Eventually the actual incidents have become embedded in a different product in which they constitute the minority of the writing. Overall, the whole account is a good example of how essential it is to use an incident to illustrate general and abstract reflection.

This next incident is rather different in that, although the teacher is similarly thematically linking different incidents, these did not just happen, but were deliberately created by the teacher herself through experimental teaching.

Incident 45: Dirty dancing

I have noticed during TV and radio broadcasts that if something out of the ordinary or 'funny' or 'rude' comes up, fairly frequently the kids will turn around and look for my reaction before they continue with their own. For example, recently there was a programme on 'Movement' which showed children doing rhythmic exercises wearing fairly revealing body-stockings. The children kind of gasped and then I saw all the heads turn round in the dark to look at me to see how I reacted.

The first time it came on I made some comment about how beautifully one could move in a suit like that, and 'I wonder how they would put them on?' The children watched silently and with great interest – giving suggestions about how they could put them on and saying how good all the muscles looked through the costumes. The second time it came on (a week later) the kids looked at me again and this time I looked shocked and commented on how I didn't think this was very suitable for a children's programme. The whole of that particular session was greeted with giggles and 'rude' comments.

So how much do I influence their reactions and values? To what extent would these hold in different situations with different people? How important is it that I keep my values the same from day to day – or would it be 'happier' for the kids if I didn't always force the same things on them as far as reactions and values are concerned? How different is what they get in school from what they are exposed to at home? Is this difference (if there is one) confusing to them?

But I will also carry this a bit further by telling them what I think they're doing. On a future occasion after the session I will ask the kids questions to find out whether their overt physical reactions actually match their mental reactions, or perhaps whether they thought my judgements were fair.

This account shows the teacher coupling incidents in an inquiring fashion after four months' writing critical incidents. There was also an earlier incident in her file which had made her sensitive to the way the students constantly looked to her to know how they should respond and react, and this naturally gave her some cause for concern. Quite unexpectedly she suddenly found that she had a very simple way of collecting more data on this problem, of sharing it with her students, and involving them in planning change. Of course, one cannot always teach experimentally, particularly if it leads to confusion and anxiety. However, what this teacher is doing in a small but ongoing way is constantly to scrutinise an aspect of her classroom practice, and to do so in such a way that it provides her with data to enable her to be more effective in understanding her judgement and changing her actions.

CONCLUSION

One could go on with such examples almost indefinitely, but the small selection here does show the basic process and possibilities of critical incident writing for practising teachers, in-service educators and academics.

Several main points may be worth repeating here. First, critical incidents usually need to be transformed for presenting to different audiences. In this case I changed many of the original incidents in two ways: (a) I took embryonic critical incidents from teachers' files and expanded the analysis in order to demonstrate the process of moving from description to diagnosis and interpretation; and (b) I relocated them in themes of my construction in order to demonstrate the value of breaking the chronological constraints of the journal form. In so doing I also showed how it is possible for someone to produce a report which incorporates the work of others.

Chapter 7

Autobiographical incidents and classroom practice

Interactive studies must be complemented by attempts to conceptualise the links between interactions and changing social structures in such a way as to point to new kinds of research which at present seem almost wholly lacking.

(Young 1971: 5)

INTRODUCTION: KINDS OF AUTOBIOGRAPHICAL INCIDENT

This is the first of two chapters on special kinds of critical incidents aimed at different kinds of understanding: biographical and political. This chapter concerns the historical dimension of teaching: how knowing something about what has happened to us and what we have done, tells us something about who and where we are, and where we might be going. This book began with an autobiographical incident about the teacher–student differences in what is interesting and valuable knowledge. I related a particular moment of insight when I became aware that I had failed to identify in my teaching the very problem that I was telling other teachers to identify in theirs. It has been an important incident for me as the initial expression of an underlying concern that has directed my work since then. That incident has been a kind of a touchstone for me throughout the writing of this book, for instance, for I have frequently returned to it to judge what I am doing and to remember what I am trying to achieve.[1] That is one important use of autobiographical critical incidents, and I will return to other aspects of it in conclusion.

In Chapter 2 I mentioned that the term 'critical incident' comes originally from history where it refers to some event or situation which marked some significant turning-point or change in the life of the subject. But I left this idea there, and went on to show how the term could also be used in the sense of making something that had hitherto appeared normal and natural, critical by showing how it exemplified underlying patterns and values. The majority of the examples presented thus far is of this latter kind. But I want here to return to autobiographical critical incidents which, because they too are of several different kinds, required a separate chapter.

In general, autobiographical critical incidents tend to be of two types, neither of which are without problems. The most obvious kind is those that are easily recalled, often in spite of having occurred many years ago. We can easily recall these for two reasons: they have an unusually high emotional charge, and they have a continuing significance. The high emotional charge ensures that the incidents always remain with us in spite of everything else that we experience over the years; we cringe or stand tall when we touch them in memory. Others are remembered more because they are significant in other, often essentially technical ways. These we tend to recount frequently, thus renewing the memory. They become 'war stories' as we use them to illustrate favourite points we are making, or just to remind ourselves of particular categories of experience: things we should or should not do, things that were fun or successful, that were quintessential in one way or another.

With the other main kind of incident, precisely the opposite occurs: we forget them. Again, these tend to be of two kinds; there are those that are forgotten simply because they were unremarkable and therefore unmemorable, and those that are not easily remembered because they are so highly charged that we cannot bear to live with them. The former we have to dredge up from the sedimented trivia beneath which they lie; and the latter we have to disinter from the sarcophagi in which we had hoped to lay them forever to rest.

Having seen the possibility of these last two kinds whilst drafting this chapter, I wondered why it was that I could not remember any. I decided the reason I could not recall any trivia was that the things I could recall I had remembered because they were highly significant in some way or other and so were not in fact commonplace at all. Similarly, the important incidents I had suppressed could only be resurrected with the help of an outsider or through another, mediating, incident, because I had buried them. These kinds are therefore particularly difficult to write about because, if they are actually trivial, they are probably not worth writing about; but if they are genuine resurrected ghosts, then we hesitate to render them material anyway.

From a methodological view, therefore, historical critical incidents are a problem, and not just because of the distortions that occur in memory, reconstruction and analysis. We all tend to consider ourselves experts on our own past, and tend to take the objectivity of our ideas about it for granted, but the processes of autobiography are complex and plagued with the usual problems of research such as reliability and validity. Again, and like all other research, outcomes vary according to the methods employed, which will in turn vary according to the interests and intentions of the researcher. We also need to bear in mind that as data critical incidents are mere fragments, minute samples of the complex plethora of everything that actually occurred. Further, they are usually highly emotionally charged and more often than not they are uncorroborated at the time and then reconstructed long afterwards.

CRITICAL INCIDENTS: FIRST- AND SECOND-HAND VALUES

Some of these points are taken up again below, so let us now move on to consider the following incident as a example of what I have so far been discussing in these rather abstract terms. It is a reasonably comfortable example of the kind of incident that I have frequently used to illustrate a point.

Incident 46: Lock-step thinking

I was taking a typical teacher-led whole class 'discussion'. We had been thinking about whether it would be a good idea or not for students to have some choice in the teachers they had. We moved onto another topic, and after about five minutes, a boy put up his hand and said, 'Well, if a teacher wasn't very much liked, then he'd know, and he'd feel sad if no one wanted to come to his class, like.'

This was one of the least able boys in a class of distinctly non-academic characters, and that was his first and only contribution to the discussion. But I, being on autopilot, responded to him by saying, 'We finished that one ages ago. Where have you been since then?'

At the time I simply thought that I had responded poorly, and decided next time to be more encouraging to the lad. And when I began writing this chapter, I chose it simply to illustrate a simple piece of learning from experience. But as I wrote it down, I could see that it was an incident which revealed a number of values and beliefs. First, I seemed to think that it was the teacher's job to judge the quality and appropriateness (timing) of a contribution, rather than to respond to the substance. Second, it implied that I wanted every student in the class to be thinking about the same thing at the same time in a discussion. Third, it showed that I valued the immediate and particular relevance of a contribution more than I valued the contributor. Very interesting, I thought, but so what? I did not really think that those were my values and beliefs at the time of the incident, and I knew they certainly were not at the time of writing. It appeared to be a simple piece of historical information, but I could not escape the contradiction between my practice and espoused values. I had been doing things I thought I did not believe in. So it nagged until I eventually asked a very important biographical question: 'Where did those values and beliefs come from?'

The answer provided a resolution to the contradiction: they came from the response itself, and not necessarily from me at all. It was a modelled reaction that I had unthinkingly absorbed from the practice of others, not an original response which I had generated from my values for myself. A whole set of values I did not then espouse, and probably never had, were embedded in the reaction and so reproduced by me. So the next biographical question I had to ask was not where did those values come from, but where did the practical response come from? Since it all occurred so long ago, I cannot be sure but I believe that the response I gave the boy was a response not infrequently given to me as a student. I could not remember specific incidents, but I can remember being reprimanded for 'not paying attention' when I was merely thinking different things about the topic instead of thinking exactly the same things that the teacher was.

Recall of that general biographical experience did not seem to help the process of my current teaching, however. Like the recognition of the values embedded in the response, I realised at the time that it was an inappropriate one, and that next time I could praise the student for persisting in thinking about a subject, or run the discussion differently. At the time I was more concerned with the technical matter of how to extend these students' thinking, and that is what I achieved. There was value in the general historical perspective and subsequent analysis, but it bore a subtle and tangential relation to the practical teaching problem. Having worked through the contradiction, I could recognise some of the values which I did espouse: I was sufficiently concerned about the student to reflect upon and recall the incident; I valued self-criticism enough to render critical a rather unremarkable incident; and I saw learning from my mistakes as being a means of growth.

Also it still is helpful to me as a teacher to understand my response as an inappropriately modelled one, for that can do two things for me: first it accounts for why the incident was so bothersome, allowing me to see myself as a reasonably whole and integrated person, one who unwittingly rather than intentionally does things which can so deeply conflict with what I think I am doing. And second, it enables me to deal with another continuing worry: the extent to which I am forever at the mercy of my past. I can accept that there are past experiences which tend to determine what I now do, because I can see also that my 'good sense' (Giroux 1983) will enable me to recognise what is happening if I am watchful about them. That enables me to feel in control again, and so, instead of cringing and writing off the incident as yet another failure, the biographical explanation leaves me feeling successful for having recognised an imposition from my past, and more hopeful about overcoming them in the future.

So this example shows that one can learn as much (if not more) from a subsequent biographical analysis as one can learn from the incident at the time. Directly from the initial enactment I learned that I not only had to change that particular response, but that I had to be vigilant about all such responses that seemed to oppose what I was trying to achieve. That recognition became absorbed into what is often called 'craft knowledge', that is, experientially derived, seldom articulated, but constantly and consistently acted upon. This whole incident (which has become something of a saga) indicates some of the power and richness of autobiography: such an analysis can transform an incident which was not even particularly important at the time it occurred into one which is important for the subject for all time.[2]

This kind of autobiography involves working back in time from an account of our current practice towards aspects of its genesis, not simply to know where it came from (though that is necessary), but to use that knowledge to change ourselves and our current practice. When working in that way, one is not aiming to produce complete, holistic personal histories, as many academics do, but a very fragmented and discontinuous account of only certain parts of the past which is, nevertheless, directly relevant to current practice. There is no one correct form of history; forms are more or less appropriate to purposes. Here one's primary aim is to deal effectively with the parts of the past that are present in our current practice.

CRITICAL INCIDENTS: RECOVERY OF THE PAST AS A JUSTIFICATION OF THE PRESENT

Incident 46: *Lock-step thinking* was a new reworking of something that happened a long time ago in my teaching career. The process of reworking is something which is itself problematical, and to which I return later in this chapter. For the second incident I will take one that happened in the morning of the afternoon that I was writing this section.

Incident 47: Teaching ideology

As we left the room after my Introduction to the Study of Language class this morning, I noticed a usually prompt student had not handed in her assignment. I asked if she had it, but she was evasive and seemed worried. I assumed that she was behind with her work, and so I said, 'By the end of the week, OK?' and thought to leave it at that.

But she came to me in the corridor a few minutes later and she said, 'I don't know what you mean by ideology'. My immediate impulse was to make the 'Where have you been all this semester?' response, but I recalled my own initial (and, let's face it, continuing) problem with the term, and paused to think. I realised that with this class I had probably come in at too high a level of understanding in my use and explanation of ideology, and I had not checked on the students' understanding of it other than with the rhetorical, 'Everyone got it?'

The fact that we had been dealing with the notion throughout the term as if all the students had come into the course with a basic idea of what it meant, had probably prevented a student who was rather shy from asking about something the tutor and all the other students seemed to take for granted as understood.

But three sessions from the end of the course she had an assignment to do which required an understanding of the term; she could hardly then ask openly in class what it meant without owning up to not having been very clear about large chunks of the course; on the other hand, if she didn't find out, she'd fail the assignment. 'OK', I said, 'let's just look at it as false consciousness and hidden valuings...'.

Afterwards I wondered whether I was correct to give such a limited account of the term. I found I could not recall how I had come to my understanding of ideology, but I could recall very clearly just where my understanding of another difficult term 'cultural capital' began. That was through an incident when I was trying to read Bourdieu and look after my youngest child. She knocked the xylophone she was playing with off the table, and in putting all the bits back I suddenly realised that the way in which I defined the task, and the way in which I was interacting with her, were actively producing cultural capital. I have used the account I wrote of the incident on many later occasions in my teaching, and once in my writing (Hodge and Tripp 1986: 174), because I have found that it is often through interpreting concrete examples of real experiences according to such notions, that one can acquire the necessary base upon which to build towards a proper understanding of abstract terms.

In view of a colleague's criticism of the approach, I began thinking about whether I was right to deal with ideology in those terms, and I recalled a concrete example I had for hegemony, and the criticism it produced. Not infrequently, I use the following (typical and actual) conversation I once observed:

Incident 48: Hegemony

Mother providing three drinks for her three children, but having only one small and two ordinary glasses. To her youngest who goes to take one of the larger ones:

No, Julie, this is yours. (*Points to smallest*)
Want big one.
No, those are for John and Mary. You have this one.
Want big one. (*Threatening a scene*)
But this is a special little one for you. I got you this glass specially. Just for you. Look, it's different from the others. It's a special one, just for you.
Child takes smallest glass.

Now that is hardly the kind of account of hegemony one finds in textbooks, and when I first presented it to a colleague, I was told in no uncertain terms that it was quite wrong to pretend that such important and complex notions could be reduced to such an example. Yet I have found that it is precisely the kind of account that makes immediate and recognisable sense to many students when faced with a definition such as: 'Hegemony has to do with the way the powerful persuade the oppressed to participate in their own oppression'. So although I saw she had a point, I was not going to give up such an apparently effective approach: rather I sought to justify it. I fell back, therefore, not only on my own previous experience with learning and teaching about such ideas, but on Bruner's notions of a spiral curriculum and the provision of 'a courteous translation'. Taken together, they suggest that a process of successive approximation towards, and increasing complexity of, knowledge is a legitimate route to understanding. The important point in that process being that the simple version should be 'intellectually honest', that it should never have to be unlearned, but only be seen differently in the light of further understanding. The incident of the child with the glasses seemed to fulfil that criterion with regard to hegemony, so I have continued to use it.

The role of biography here is clear: when in doubt I used aspects of my professional biography (critical incidents, tried and trusted explanations and significant others) in at least four ways: to inform, evaluate, approve and to justify how I dealt with the current problem. Going over the incident within an hour of its occurrence reconfirmed for me that facilitating understanding through that process is and should remain an important aspect of my personal theory of teaching.

A further point in all this is that tracing the history of a practice in order to understand and question it should not always lead to change: if we are reasonably successful teachers we will get things fairly right much of the time. So a reconsideration will usually approve and confirm our current practice rather than change it. If changes are to occur as the result of this kind of evaluation and 'recertification' of a practice, then they are likely to be an extension of a successful practice into other less successful situations. In this case, I decided that when teaching the same course next year, I would spend at least one session on defining ideology, and that I would start to collect other simple and concrete examples (like those I have for hegemony and cultural capital) to illustrate ideology. The result was the list of ways of being 'fair' in Chapter 4.

CRITICAL INCIDENTS AS 'WAR STORIES'

As I have pointed out throughout this book, we all have adopted, adapted and built up mental constructs about our practice, and, wittingly or not, we adopt and express values consciously or through the practices we employ. These constructs and values are generally implicit in what we do, rather than being overt and consciously articulated. When we come up against them, however, it is often in dramatic ways. This kind of critical incident might better be termed, 'war stories'. As staffroom conversation bears witness, we all have a stock of these 'war stories', and many of them have a kind of moral which has affected our current practice in very obvious ways. For instance, one of mine is about homework.

Incident 49: Homework

I was teaching in an English grammar school where homework was considered to be so important that failing to do it was punished by lunch-hour detention. In one class (13–14-year-olds) there was one girl called Mandy whose class-work was good, but whose homework was usually poorly done, and sometimes not done at all. I always seemed to be sending her to detention. One evening after school I was sitting in the staff room with some colleagues when the school secretary put her head round the door, and seeing me, asked if, when I went home, I could give a lift to a girl who had missed her bus. In the hallway I met Mandy.

Missed your bus?

Yeah.

That's just typical, isn't it? You not only can't do your homework, but you can't even get sufficiently well organised to catch your bus. OK then, what happened?

Went shopping.

You went downtown? You know that it's not only against the rules to go shopping after school, but you should also know that you've not time to get there and back and catch the bus. What'd you go there for anyway?

Had to get some meat.

Why did you have to get the meat? Doesn't your mother do the shopping?

No, Mum's gone away.

Sorry to hear that. But if you knew you had to get the meat, why didn't you get a chit from your tutor and go in the lunch hour?

'Cos you sent me to homework detention.

And as we drove home the story emerged. Mandy's parents had split up when Dad met Joy. Mum had moved to another town with Bill, but the children (Mandy 13, and the twins, 9), had stayed with their father and Joy so that they could all continue in the same schools. They spent most weekends and the holidays with Mum and Bill. Mandy liked that, they had a pony there. But Dad was a commercial traveller who was often away for up to three nights a week. Joy had left Dad, and Mandy's Gran, who had lived in the same village, had died a few weeks ago. Not only was Mandy having to cope with the considerable pressure of grammar school work and competition, not only had her family broken up and her grandmother died just as she was entering adolescence, but at 13 she was looking after her younger twin brothers alone for several nights a week. And I had put her in detention for not completing her homework.

The following day in class, Mandy had not done her homework again. I said nothing, but was about to send another student to detention for the same thing when he asked why I was sending him but not Mandy, who'd offended two days in a row. I said I'd found out that she had enough problems on her hands, and so I wasn't going to make her do homework for the rest of the term. I asked the class if they thought that I was being unfair by making an exception, and discovered not only that they agreed with my action, but that they already knew of her situation, and they had been helping her by doing her homework for her in other subjects. Unfortunately, the kind of work I was setting in English meant that she alone could do it, which was why she had been caught.

This traumatic experience made a great impression on me, particularly as I had only been teaching for eighteen months. There is no doubt that I have since mythologised it in order to make it a more comfortable reference point in my thought, but at the time it raised some immediate issues. I was forced to challenge some of the beliefs and theories upon which I had been acting. First, did the idea of being 'fair' mean (a) treating all students exactly alike regardless of individual differences, and (b) being consistent? This was something I had always accepted in my own schooling, and had felt pressured into by my students (as the challenge to my action showed). It was, however, neither necessary nor true: we all saw the need for exceptions, and accepted them happily. Second, I found that I could share my teaching decisions with my students: they were responsible negotiators, and clearly had rules and rights to negotiate. Third, I found that one teaches people not subjects, and that, contrary to expectations resulting from an education for teaching consisting principally of a three year degree in English literature, I had to learn my students and forget much of my subject. I also learned that the pastoral support system of the school could, and often did, break down... and there must have been other things that I learned too, but which I have not yet recovered. Such an experience was formative in that it left me a quite different teacher in some respects afterwards. Not only did it impact on a specific classroom practice, but I also realised that routines needed critical evaluation, which was a change in my professional awareness.

CRITICAL INCIDENTS AS TURNING-POINTS

To work on the past in such ways might be to run against the canons of historiography, because critical incidents were but a small class of the many incidents which would be recounted in an essentially holistic approach. They were necessarily a small class because they were critical in the sense that they were turning-points in people's lives, points at which people sought new directions, changed their jobs or opinions, changed their social, personal or material circumstances, and so on. Such points are not always very obvious to the person at the time, and others may have become so repressed and hidden that they are not easily recovered by willed conscious recall alone. In such instances a therapeutic 'critical friend' can be a great help, and the teacher–educator or researcher engaged in working with teachers on their biographies will often find themselves playing that role. However, biography is not something that necessarily needs the assistance of an outsider: though the view of a 'critical friend' is often very helpful, it is not difficult to perform the process unaided. It is mainly in order to demonstrate the point that all the examples in this section are taken from my own teaching which I have analysed for and by myself. They are not, therefore, the kind of incidents which I have repressed, though I did repress certain aspects of the first incident for some years.

We have already looked at an incident which was critical in the sense that when it was analysed and worked through, it became invested with new meaning which was transformative of understanding and practice. But none of them have been critical in the sense of their being turning-points in a person's life, which is the way in which most biographers use the term. I now want to discuss such an incident, choosing one from my professional life which also serves to illustrate that mental events also constitute powerful critical incidents which can influence subsequent life choices quite as dramatically as the most newsworthy public event. Such a mental event may be simply an occasion when a number of events, though small in themselves, suddenly fall into a greater, totally new and massively transforming pattern from which an entirely new view of ourselves or the situation emerges. Hudson recognised this possibility when he wrote:

The vital moments in human development and their tell-tale signs, are not always, and perhaps not ever, well-advertised affairs, detectable with bold questions and simple-minded tests. There may be nothing more than subtle shifts in our feeling about the people around us and the ideas within us. It is with these seemingly slight details, redolent of who we think we are and what we would like to become, that the study of intellectual growth must come to terms.

(Hudson 1972: 114)

That is as true of professional development as it is of intellectual. Some casual remark or apparently insignificant event raises problems, makes us see or understand something, or suddenly clarifies everything. The following traditional kind of 'turning-point' critical incident is both like that and more like the case I imagine Hudson had in mind. It occurred on a very ordinary occasion: morning recess in the staffroom.

Incident 50: Career paths

As I sat to one side thankfully sipping the revolting staffroom coffee, I suddenly saw things very differently, but quite clearly. Amongst the staff were two groups of old men, one doing the football pools and another doing *The Times* crossword in about 12 minutes flat; almost all of them were excellent teachers. But there was a younger mixed group of less-experienced teachers discussing a series of staff–student lunch-hour games they were arranging. I'd done it for the previous two years and was leaving it to others this year. I had other, more important things to do as a housemaster. At the time I was considering going for a head of department position, when suddenly I saw a lifetime of unbroken teaching as a kind of inverted funnel in which the further one went the narrower and less involved one became with the children one was teaching. In that image I could see why it was that the old men and the young mixed group were as they were, and not the other way around. Rather than the football pools, I'd probably be doing the crossword in twenty years' time, but either way, as evidenced by the importance I was now attaching to administration, my priorities and concerns were unlikely to remain with the children I taught.

Until that moment I had never thought to do anything with my life except be a classroom teacher; but after that my next move was to go farming for two years before teaching again, and later doing various other things, like research and lecturing. One might think that the fact that I saw those people in that way at that time, and myself and my life in relation to them, has nothing to do with the specifics of my professional practice. But that insight still affects the way in which I approach teachers: is this person still engaged with their teaching, or is it merely a habitual way of earning a living? In an education system with very little growth, how can I help this teacher to accept the fact that their prospects for promotion or change are dismally small in the foreseeable future, and still enable them to remain growing people professionally and personally? Such feelings that define how I see other people are not only anchored in my own thoughts and experiences, but they constantly emerge as constructs that determine the kind of work which I am interested in, and the way in which I go about it. Readers could perhaps make other quite different connections (of which I am entirely unaware) between my account of these experiences and the design of this book, for instance.

SIGNIFICANT OTHERS

Such changes in consciousness as evidenced in the last example emphasise the importance of recognising the features that we have consciously espoused or constructed for ourselves and which are therefore uniquely ours, and features that it would appear we have taken from, or which have been imposed upon us by others, or which are embedded in certain ideas or practices which we have adopted. In the first category are, for instance, our values, beliefs and the personal experiences that have been formative in that we have willingly changed by learning from them; in the second are both the values embedded in the practices we have uncritically adopted, and also other aspects of our professional history and position, such as our role as defined by the school, the social and psychological theories we have espoused and the views, rules and dictates of significant others (principals, colleagues, spouses, students). So in examining our personal and professional histories for explanations of our teaching we must consider the way in which what we do and what we have become is at least partly determined by the social and material conditions of our professional practice.

In the last example, as I encountered the problem at the time it was less a product of my own values than of my having uncritically accepted a role determined for me by the common practice of the school in which I taught. Later it became an incident which I could see informed many aspects of my teaching, and as such can be said to be critical in the historical sense. Critical incidents which are subsequently recovered by a process of introspection are used to build up practice-specific aspects of a personal–professional history; and the incidents as they were analysed at the time not only compose that history but can be used to recover it.

When using a critical incident approach to our histories there is a danger that we become mesmerised and captivated by the drama of our more powerful experiences. It is important, therefore, also to consider other, more subtle forms of influence, such as the impact of other people upon our values and practices. That means a re-consideration of our professional education in terms of the people, the significant others (in education or not), the friends, tutors, co-operating teachers, advisers and principals, who in one way or another changed the way we think about ourselves and our practice.

Different people taught us by their example, by the theorists they acquainted us with through the literature, by the courses they ran. They influenced our thinking not only directly through 'teaching', but also indirectly through who they themselves were, how they saw and represented the world, and what we saw in them.

There are probably several such people with whom we are still in contact in one way or another. In my case, I can recall three people who have played a significant role in my professional life. First, there was a new English teacher who gave me full marks for a story which had a great many spelling mistakes. Every other teacher before had taken half-a-mark off for each mistake and made me write it out three times, so I had learned to write as little as possible. I still cannot spell, but I do enjoy writing, and I can remember thinking that if one can really do that kind of thing as a teacher, teaching might be a good thing to do.

Then there are two who have been most influential in my current work, the late Bill Joesbury, my undergraduate philosophy tutor from whom I learned amongst other things the critical stance to the taken-for-granted which has become so much a part of me and so important to my work; and Bob Hodge, a colleague with whom I work and who first introduced me to critical linguistics and semiotics. Then there are others whom I have never known in such a personal way: the 'reconceptualist' school of curriculum theorists who I have come to know more through their published writings than through direct contact. To discover the kind of influences such people have upon us, it is necessary not only to identify them and their theories, but to examine the values, assumptions and beliefs embedded in their views and how they continue to influence us.

We are always selective in how much of what we take from others, and that can sometimes cause contradictions. If, for instance, we take Piaget to heart, in doing so we will tend to see children as using cognitive operations which are essentially different to those of adults, and we will tend to consider formal thinking as the apogee of the human intellect. But if we reject those aspects of Piaget whilst accepting his view of 'construction', then that also affects our professional judgement and tells us things about the way in which we practice. Similarly, if we examine our view of what our immediate superior values and encourages, we may find we tend to maximise and bring into the open the aspects that we too agree with, and we tend to ignore, covertly oppose or subvert those aspects with which we disagree. In such ways many people have a very direct impact upon our professional judgement, the effects of which we need to examine if we are going to control them for ourselves.

RECORDING, RESHAPING AND VERIFICATION

With all the examples in this chapter I have worked through what is perhaps the easiest way into our personal histories: introspection. At its simplest, a professional history is merely a matter of looking for precedents as a response to the question, 'Why did (do) I do that?' It is something anyone can do for themselves. Because teaching is in many ways a very routine activity, we can often recall other similar occasions from which we learned to respond in a particular way to a current event. What we are trying to do by recording thoughts and events is move beyond the purely practical, 'This happened, so I must do that' to the diagnostic, 'I think this happened because of that and so what must I do about what happened and its cause?' It is in accounting for 'what happened' that we have to take into account both the social and material conditions of our practice and also who we are; and it is that aspect which inevitably creeps into the record.

A written account of these things is important, because having a record to examine encourages us to analyse it in a deeper and more objective way that we tend to avoid when we spontaneously recall past thoughts or events within the usual flow of our daily lives. The written account not only facilitates and formalises our telling or retelling of them, but simultaneously encourages and records the way we inevitably reshape the experience, highlighting or suppressing features according to how we are feeling about them when writing. This is entirely natural and useful, because in the reshaping we allow our subconscious to write in things which we may recognise as important only after they have appeared on paper. Part of that reshaping is the result of re-analysis which might, as in the first example above, occur a very long time later. The point is that if the incident and our thoughts about it are recorded, then it is always available for reworking, and it is surprising how often I have reworked incidents in the course of preparing them for publication.

For instance, I originally wrote Incident 46: *Lock-step thinking*, nearly fifteen years ago for an evaluation report. I copied it a decade later for teaching materials, and then again eighteen months after that for this chapter. In the first write-up and copying I thought that the values I expressed must have been my values because I had expressed them; it was only when re-analysing it that I saw that the expressed values were not values I espoused, but second-hand values which I had inherited through the use of an unproblematised response. That there was such a gap between the incident and subsequently working it through does not invalidate the re-analysis, though the delay was a pity in view of the fact that I had been bothered by it all that time. It was only the re-analysis that enabled me to lay to rest the initial feelings of failure. In doing this kind of revision, one is adopting the relativistic stance of modern historiography in which alternative and re-interpretations are seen not just as inevitable, but as necessary. Traditional notions of what makes 'good' historical interpretation simply do not apply: as Homberger and Charmley (1988) put it, 'There can never be definitive biography, merely a version'. One is therefore actively encouraging the author's subjectivities to appear in the text, and to generate successive provisional accounts.[3] A teacher's autobiography is never done.

The analysis of critical incidents is not a once-off and final affair, then, but an on-going one in which new links can constantly be made, not only to current practice, but to how we see ourselves in relation to current and past selves and practices. There is, of course, a danger here in that I may have used my current understanding as a 'platform for hindsight' (Walker 1980), replacing a (correct) earlier analysis with a later (incorrect, but more comfortable) one, so that the original incident is made to appear consonant with the subsequent discovery. In this case, who is to say whether I did or did not actually espouse the values expressed? The idea that I had used a modelled reaction which contained values at odds with those I currently espoused, is a diagnosis which cannot be supported by the evidence of this incident alone. Other evidence of a more obviously biographical and psychological nature needs to be brought to bear to verify it.

In that regard, the existence of the original written record is one guard against misrepresentation: one can check other aspects of the record to discover what one was doing and thinking at the time, and whether the new view accords with other instances in the record, or whether there are so many counter-instances that there is more compelling evidence for the original analysis. One can also see where that later interpretation came from. The temporal difference, however, does not invalidate the analysis, rather it strengthens it: it suggests a continuous and coherent emergence of an idea which one has been working towards. In other words, without the earlier incident the later understanding may never have occurred. A critical friend is a great help in such a process, and it is often only the record which allows us to share the experience and analysis with others who can point out things which they can see, and which we can then take into consideration for ourselves.

With regard to the psychological check, it is plausible to suggest that it was probably the contradiction in values which made such an apparently routine incident sufficiently salient to force my attention to it. In fact, I would hazard a guess that in every instance where our actions have concerned, shamed or embarrassed us at the time, or we have cringed to recall them later, our actions have expressed values which are contradictory to those which we consciously espoused and subscribed to. In such incidents the contemporary written record not only prevents us repressing the memory of the incident, but establishes how we saw the incident at the time, which is an important part of the record. In this instance, I wrote merely that this was an example of the difficulty of pacing a teacher led thinking session with a heterogeneous class. That expressed a concern more with the technical aspect of my teaching: I did not mention values, hidden or otherwise, at the time. Nevertheless, it was the contradiction in values which made the incident so salient, because, thinking back over my then recent teaching, I could see a number of other incidents in which the same technical difficulty was apparent, which had passed entirely unnoticed and unrecorded at the time. That I dealt with it at a technical level at the time is typical of the practical problematic, and in some ways a protective response.

A real danger of the approach outlined is that, uncritically used, critical incidents and critical incident file accounts of our espoused theories, have great and compelling explanatory power, the conservative force of which should not be underestimated: 'I did not insist on Jim handing in his homework, because I remember when...'; 'Piaget says that there is no point in giving them questions like that when they are at the concrete operations stage...'; 'Children need to be told what they can and cannot do, they cannot learn self-discipline until they have learned to obey someone else...'; 'I use stars and stamps because saying something like "good work" is so vague. I always put a stamp on work that is good, it really shows them it is good...'. We often make and hear such statements about our teaching as if they were final and complete justifications for our actions. Constant re-analysis is important, for unless one deliberately reconsiders the previous record, it is all too easy to accept incidents without challenge or critique, in which case one begins to write a history which simply confirms present practices: 'This is what I did; I see it like this; and as it felt OK, I shall just go on with it.'

So, rather than accepting our initial versions of critical incidents, we should use our accounts to alert us to the possibility of unrecognised values. In particular, others may find our analysis partial, ill-informed or outright wrong; and the explanations we favour indicate much deeper underlying mental constructs that we value. As I suggested earlier, facts seldom challenge values: we ignore, reinterpret or find other facts when certain facts appear to challenge our values. If we are going to challenge our use of past experience and significant others, then we need to do so in terms both of the accuracy of the facts and in terms of the values we express through them. That is really only likely to happen if one makes any and all analysis provisional, reworking data so that one aims less for conclusions and explanations which are constant over time, more at hypotheses and viewpoints which are always emergent, revisable and open to transformation. In terms of understanding the basis of our professional judgement, it is important to allow and facilitate that process.

CONCLUSION

In this chapter I have tried to develop aspects of one of the main themes of this book, that working on our professional practice is always and necessarily a matter of working on the values in the practice, rather than working on the practice itself. Whether it is an incident with a boy contributing a comment when he is ready, or a girl not doing homework, it is only by attending to the values that are exposed by the incident that it is possible to achieve a sufficiently deep diagnosis to move beyond the practical problematic and into other kinds of professional judgement. What is so important in personal professional autobiography is the ongoing recognition, articulation, critique and modification of our values. Far from being end-points, then, the recall and historical analysis of critical incidents should constitute departure points for our reflection and understanding.

In its more traditional forms, educational biography has enjoyed something of a renaissance in the last ten years, which is encouraging as it can overcome some of the problems of the exclusion of the viewpoint of teachers that occurs in other forms of research.[4] But one difference between most of the life history studies and the approach illustrated here is that most educational biographers use the incidents in a teacher's personal and professional history to explain the origin of current values, judgements and practices in their teaching. In the process those values, judgements and practices are seldom examined in other ways or challenged. In contrast, teachers tend to work the other way around, from observations of present teaching practices to the biographical critical incidents that lie behind them. In the approach taken in this chapter it is professional judgement in classroom practice which is paramount. So although critical incidents may be the primary source of data in most life history work, they are not necessarily dealt with in the same way or with the same purpose in mind.

To insist on the primacy of practice is not to decry the enormous value of knowing in a holistic, coherent and comprehensive way about ourselves, of understanding how and why we have become the kinds of people and teachers that we are, of revealing the whole 'architecture of self', as Pinar (1986) puts it. A whole biography is important when dealing with the values which impinge on our teaching because it can reveal aspects of practice that we could not otherwise have recognised. But so also, examining incidents in our practice reveals things about our biographies that we would not otherwise be able to recall. In both approaches we are seeking the presence of the past as a way of illuminating, articulating, understanding and gaining control over our professional development, judgement and practice.

It is always tempting for academics to continue to work exclusively with the recognised and accepted methods. But we should not constrain what we can learn from our past or how we could use those understandings by limiting our approach to what a particular tradition of historical scholarship enables us to do. Young's (1971: 5) observation quoted at the start of this chapter draws attention to the fact that we need to invent new forms of scholarship to service our professional needs, and perhaps the kind of autobiographical critical incident created by the analysis of practice is a possibility. It is important that the purposes and interests of teachers determine the nature of educational historical method, not the other way around.

Finally returning to the first autobiographical incident mentioned in this book in the Afterthought, it is interesting that the creation of a critical incident from something that happened in my life has in turn created something in my life. What I recognised in my teaching through that teacher's letter on students' knowledge, changed the direction of my professional work and led to this book. And by continually referring to it when writing I have consciously incorporated an aspect of my past into my future. That is another major difference between traditional forms of autobiography and the critical incident approach outlined here. The former is usually produced towards the end of a person's life (almost invariably after retirement) and primarily as an account for others; but here we have autobiography occurring and re-occurring throughout the whole of a teacher's working life; and rather than its being an account for their interest, it is something they can use to shape their personal and professional lives.

Chapter 8

Socially critical action and analysis[1]

INTRODUCTION: CRITICAL THEORY

Here I want to explore further the idea of a critical incident analysis that is social in what it critiques and how one critiques it. The idea of the analysis is to raise questions about how people should behave towards each other in a socially just society. Such a specific idea will often challenge the judgements and values revealed by general reflection. In the literature the approach is often called 'critical' because it comes from what has been called 'critical theory', but to distinguish the approach from the many other ways in which one can be critical, I shall use the term 'socially critical'. However, although I want to use some socially critical ideas, I cannot pretend to deal with much of what has become a huge and still rapidly growing literature. So rather than attempting a comprehensive account of critical theory, I shall instead merely point to and summarise the few selected features that I regard as essential. The way I shall do this is to begin with a definition and some of its implications, and then use the approach on an incident in order to see what kind of changes to practice are suggested. This I shall do through a very brief analysis of an incident and the teacher's reflection upon it. First, then to a very short account of some aspects of critical theory.

The term 'critical theory' is used to refer to the work of a group of socio-political analysts commonly referred to as 'The Frankfurt School', whose prominent members included Theodore Adorno, Herbert Marcuse and more recently, Jürgen Habermas. They were all interested in the idea of a more just society in terms, not just of all people having equal access to the good things of life, but also and perhaps more importantly, of people being in cultural, economic and political control of their lives. They argued that these goals could only be achieved through 'emancipation', a process by which oppressed and exploited people became sufficiently 'empowered' to transform their circumstances for themselves by themselves. It is called 'critical theory' because they saw the route to emancipation as being a kind of self-conscious and rational critique which calls into question all social relations, in particular those of and within the discursive practices of power, especially, for Habermas, technical rationalism.

Aspects of this work have been taken into education in a number of different ways, but most notably by Paulo Freire (1972) in his work with oppressed minorities which gave rise to the term 'critical pedagogy' meaning teaching–learning from within the principles of critical theory. Henry Giroux (1983) and Michael Apple (1982) and Shirley Grundy (1987) amongst others have provided comprehensive, accessible and succinct accounts of the nature and working of critical theory in their work on the political, institutional and bureaucratic control of knowledge, learners and teachers.[2]

Another group to use critical theory in education comprises those working in action research, a movement which has been particularly strong in Australia, largely initiated as it was by Stephen Kemmis of Deakin University and developed by others, particularly Shirley Grundy and Robin McTaggart.[3] It is with this last approach that my own principal interests lie and has led to the following definition:

> Socially critical analysis in education is informed by principles of social justice, both in terms of its own ways of working and in terms of its outcomes in and orientation to the community. It involves strategic pedagogic action on the part of classroom teachers aimed at emancipation from overt and covert forms of domination. In practical terms, it is not simply a matter of challenging the existing practices of the system, but of seeking to understand what makes the system be the way it is and challenging that, whilst remaining conscious that one's own sense of justice and equality is itself open to question.
>
> (modified from Tripp 1990b 161)

Such a definition obviously begs the question of the nature of the ideal of 'social justice': whose ideal, with regard to what and based on what criteria? It is differences in these factors which result in the thirteen different ways of 'fair' distribution referred to in Chapter 4 (p. 58). Such an example shows just how difficult and subjective the notion of social justice actually is, especially in education where, in different situations and for different purposes, every one of the different kinds of allocation are used: they all represent different kinds of 'fairness', whether it is with regard to who gets how much and what kind of education, or who gets how much and what kind of attention in a lesson.

FOUR KINDS OF JUDGEMENT

In the socially critical theory literature (and its two most obvious educational offspring, critical pedagogy and critical action research,[4] one finds three different forms of practice, each informed by a different human interest. These are termed the 'technical', the 'practical' and the 'emancipatory' interests (Grundy 1982). Although these terms make good sense within Habermas's (1972) special sense, many people find them confusing because it seems that the technical and emancipatory are unpractical. I prefer to deal in different kinds of judgement rather than in kinds of practice, using the terms: practical, reflective and socially critical instead[5] and adding 'diagnostic'. This helps in two ways: one can clearly distinguish the different kinds of analysis necessary to inform each kind of judgement, and it recognises that the kind of analysis employed determines the nature of any subsequent practice.

The main difference between practical and reflective judgement is that the former is primarily concerned with the practical problematic (that is, answering the questions, 'What can I do and how best can I do it?); whereas reflection has a normatively critical problematic which asks, 'What should I do and why ought I to do it?' The forms of analysis associated with these kinds of judgement ask their questions within the constraints of the existing situation, whereas the third kind of judgement uses socially critical analysis to also question the social assumptions on which practical and reflective judgements are based. For instance, the practical tends to treat the social world as if it were part of the natural world, whereas the reflective recognises the difference between the two but accepts the social world as it is. The socially critical, however, not only recognises the difference between the natural and the social world, but critiques and seeks to improve the latter by, for instance, making it more egalitarian. As we saw in Chapter 2, however, all these kinds of judgement require a thorough understanding of what is going on, which cannot be achieved without some kind of an explanation, which is why diagnosis is also necessary and so important.

For example, a teacher has a problem with children who constantly disrupt the lesson by calling out. A purely practical analysis might result in the teacher employing a method such as a 'time out' procedure as a way to extinguish the unwanted behaviour. A diagnostic analysis would have to include some questions which were totally obviated by the first solution (such as what might be causing the unwanted behaviour); and reflective analysis could lead one to consider how one was feeling about the situation. A socially critical analysis might question the social implications of communication that was so one-way that it prevented the learners from choosing what contribution they would make and when (see Tripp 1987 for a more detailed account of this example). To do that would mean taking responsibility for normative moral issues such as who should be able to do what, when and why.

However, as others (such as Grundy 1987) have dealt very thoroughly with the nature and effects of these different interests, I shall move straight into a consideration of practice which is socially critical because it is informed by an ideal of social justice. In teaching, if our analysis is to be anything other than purely academic, it is important to make a conscious commitment to realising our social critique through changes to practice. This 'action agenda' is summarised by Livingstone (1987: 8) when he defines the aim of critical pedagogy as 'the empowerment of subordinate groups through shared understanding of the social construction of reality'. It is important to note, however, that all notions of subordination, injustice and inequality are based upon subjective assessments of empirical facts; indeed, the very idea that 'critical pedagogy' should further improvement of the lot of the least-privileged rather than, for instance, more efficient exploitation of them, is one such judgement. And, as suggested in Chapter 4, these judgements are never without their own contradictions. For instance, in terms of financial rewards, most people consider it unjust to discriminate between people upon the inherited characteristics of race, class or gender; but at the same time they consider it necessary and just to discriminate upon equally inherited mental aptitudes. The point is that the choice of grounds upon which to discriminate is always a subjective interpretation of empirical differences.

Bearing that in mind, central to socially critical practice is a two-fold critique: first, society is viewed as being essentially unjust, but capable, through rational human action, of becoming less unjust if not actually just; and second, the notions of justice and equality themselves are subjected to ideological examination. In socially critical analysis, the dominant forms of professional practice are seen to have been generated by a particular world view, set of values, and constraints, which have been constructed by certain interest groups principally for the benefit of those groups. Most obviously, one could point to aspects such as the exclusion of certain kinds of knowledge from the school curriculum, or the way the educational system is used to select certain people for certain jobs. As has been frequently documented (see, for instance, Apple 1986, and Aronowitz and Giroux 1985), the dominant professional knowledge interest in education is the technical, and it is principally that which is challenged by a social critique of teacher professionalism. The important point in socially critical professional practice is that neither social critique nor changes to professional practice are adequate without the other. In this chapter, therefore, I want to both perform an analysis and suggest the kind of action that it implies.

AN INCIDENT

At first sight, all analysis of practice by teachers might appear to be socially critical in that it tends to empower individual teachers by increasing their understanding and thereby increasing the possibility of the development of radically different practices in a professional community that is likely to challenge the existing order (Green and Reid 1986: 19). But it is important not to confuse such side-effects of critical incident analysis with an intentionally socially critical project. Teachers' professional jugements become socially critical when they become aware of the social implications of their practice and begin to work on those. That happened, for instance, when a teacher turned from asking how she could reduce the incidence of tale-telling in her classroom (Incident 57), to trying to discover how she and her colleagues had come to make gendered judgements, and what could be done about them.

Socially critical practice does not, therefore, necessitate a totally different kind of project to reflective practice at the outset, but is more a matter of incorporating into practice, diagnosis, and reflection an understanding of social context and social effects, and acting upon that context and those effects to facilitate forms of consciousness and practice which would not have been available within the initial situation or practice. In fact, in my experience few teachers set out to embark upon socially critical analysis: they tend to begin with incidents that appear to raise more obviously practical or reflective issues. They intend to deal with improving such matters as discipline, inquiry learning, extension, spelling, learning in heterogeneous classes, and so on, but they soon find that socially critical questions emerge as they proceed.

This is important because the way in which we see a situation sets our agenda for action in it. Socially critical practices therefore depend first on a critique of our existing practice in terms of the extent to which it meets our criteria of social justice, and second on our imagining how we could in future improve the match between the two. As usual, I shall do this through a teacher's critical incident.

Incident 51: Measurement

Today I conducted a lesson on measuring. It was a Grade 3 class. Predicting was involved and many of the children found it dificult to predict first. Most children went ahead and measured the item first. Constant attention and guidance was given to these children.

Another unusual thing which happened was that when they had predicted and then measured, some looked back at their prediction and crossed it out! The children didn't have to be correct. Somehow I don't think they understood the relationship between predicting and measuring.

If I could do this lesson over again, I would make the whole class go over the different stages together. A step-by-step introduction would allow the students to see that adults predict without getting the 'right' answer.

However, I must admit that there were a few children who were predicting quite well. It was obvious that these children understood the concept behind predicting and measuring, without having wild guesses.

Predicting is a very hard concept to do properly and understand. I guess a way to overcome it, is to do it informally. For example, guessing how many jelly beans in a jar. This certainly would be a good starting point.

Socially critical analysis requires a diagnosis of the incident; this account is only a description of an incident and some ideas about what to do next time; we need to know why 'many of the children found it difficult to predict first' the answer they would get from measuring. Asking 'why' necessitates a closer look at what happened, and it seems that the children did not find the actual process of making predictions difficult, but chose to measure instead of predicting. So the most obvious answer is that the children strongly believed that to do mathmatics well means getting the right answer. The description can then be checked for evidence to support or counter that hypothesis, and the way in which some of the children crossed out their predictions when they found them to be 'wrong', supports it. Further support comes from the words, 'adults predict without getting the "right" answer', for although 'right' is in quotation marks, underlying the statement is the idea that a prediction that differs from a measurement is 'wrong'. Further, 'wild guesses' imply the presence of right answers, for guesses can only be 'wild' by being too far off a 'right' answer. If this is how the teacher writes about the situation, then it is probable that these mixed messages would have undermined the effect of the teacher's saying to the children that 'right' answers were not important.

PRACTICAL IMPLICATIONS

We now need to follow and unite two different strands in this analysis: one the social implications and the other the practical implications. As will become clear in this and the next section, socially critical ideas of justice are equally important to the analysis of both aspects. Dealing with the practical implications first, it is reasonable to assume that these Grade 3 children were not trying to thwart the teacher's intentions by deliberately doing the 'wrong' thing, but had misunderstood her. This means that what the children thought the teacher wanted them to do differed from what the teacher actually wanted them to do. Again, we need to check this hypothesis out with the account, and it seems that she agrees in that she thinks it would be useful for her to also show them what they should do because they have not understood the instructions (predict first) or some necessary fact (the prediction–measurement relation). We can also bring other knowledge to bear to explain the situation, and in this case I would suggest that the problem arose because the children had already had some practice at estimation, and did not realise that prediction was something different. One can therefore agree with the teacher's recognition that the children should have been prepared for this activity in a different kind of way, but I would disagree with her suggestion as to what that preparation should have involved, particularly the use of the bean jar for the introduction to a lesson on predicting.

My reason for this lies in her writing that in order to make sure the children do it correctly next time she would first 'go over the different stages' with the class in order to show them that 'adults predict without getting the "right" answer'. This suggests that, although she recognised that the 'right answer syndrome' was a problem here (further support for my original diagnosis), she saw it as a management problem (they must follow this routine) and as a lack of knowledge (they should know adults do not 'get it right' either). In spite of her having given 'constant attention and guidance ... to these children', it was this combination of factors which resulted in the children not knowing what they should be doing.

There is a curious circularity there: prediction, the idea that she says they did not understand sufficiently well to perform the activity, is the very thing they were supposed to learn through performing the activity. What seems to have happened here, then, is that her 'theory-in-use' is one in which children learn through wanting to follow her instructions (rather than by knowing what it is they want to learn), and that this did not work well because she inadvertently set an activity in which an understanding not already possessed by all the children was required to perform it.

Although she recognises that they did not understand what they were supposed to be learning ('I do not think they understood the relationship between predicting and measuring'), what she omits from this account is a consideration of the children's relationship to their learning. That is a very significant absence from both a political and a pedagogical point of view, for I would suggest that there is a subtle and covert kind of domination of learners here that actually hinders their learning and disempowers them as (future) learners. It is clear that the learning strategy being offered to these children is to do what the teacher tells them without knowing what they should be learning; and although that does not mean it is a strategy which deprives children of actively intending to learn,[6] it is a strategy which deprives children of participation in deciding both what they intend to learn and how they intend to learn it. Thus a kind of double exclusion has occurred: first the children have been excluded from the process of making these learning decisions and they have been excluded again by not being told about them.

Returning for a moment to the methodological principles of socially critical analysis, it is for just such reasons that the questioning of our awareness is so central to the method. That the teacher saw the problem as one of the children not understanding something (and therefore needing telling) and not as one of their relationship to their learning (and therefore needing to relate to her, the task, and each other in a different way) is a matter of the problematic in use. We have already discussed problematic as the theoretical structure which causes something to be seen as a problem. The main point of the earlier discussion was how a problematic will therefore also determine the kind of information sought to provide the kind of answers which are accepted as reasonable solutions. Problematics are based on and contain particular assumptions. In this case the dominant idea of the teacher's problematic is that the most important thing in classroom learning is children's (lack of) understanding.

Note how, as they usually do, one problematic hid the absence of another here: defining the problem in one (habitual) way prevented certain other considerations. That this is so is shown by the fact that if the lesson had gone perfectly well in terms of what the children did, the teacher would not have felt there was any kind of a problem at all: how could there be a problem if classroom learning is about doing what the teacher says and the children had done it? Nevertheless, in that situation the children's relationship to their learning would still have been just as much of a problem though no problem would have been seen. The point is that there can never be a 'problem-less' situation: problems are what we think of as a problem, and what makes us think of something as a problem is our 'problematic'.

It should now be clear from the analysis that all kinds of analysis operate with different problematics, and socially critical analysis is no exception: in particular it makes a problem of social relations in terms of access, autonomy and power. Having seen that, we can now look again at what was happening in the lesson through that problematic, and we find that the construction of the activity did not maximise at least one of my principles of social justice in learning, namely that the children were not participating in the management of their own learning and were therefore being denied the opportunity to take responsibility for it (Tripp 1989). So let us now see what happens when we begin to re-plan the same lesson[7] to make the activity more socially just in my terms by making it consonant with my ideas of relevance and participation, lack of which was highlighted in my analysis. One way to do that is to let the children know and decide exactly what it is they are going to learn and why, and to give them the opportunity to work out amongst themselves and with the teacher a good way of learning it. Here is one way in which that could be done.

1 First, one would have to clarify the purpose of prediction, which is, of course, to enable one to prepare for something. One might then move on to the idea that prediction of a measurement involves estimation, the purpose of which is to check the likelihood of the measurement being correct: too wide a variation between the estimate and the measurement and one should look again to see whether the mistake is an unreasonable estimate or an inaccurate measurement.

2 The children would then have to understand three things about estimation: (a) that having verified the accuracy of the measurement one should substitute it for the estimate: (b) that estimates are different from 'guesses' because they are based on experience and some kind of evidence, such as comparison or a sample; and (c) that the only occasion when one would not substitute accurate measurement for an estimate is one in which measurement is unnecessary, is impossible or when one is practising estimation.

3 The children would then have to see why it is necessary for them to practise estimation, and (our new problematic is again important here) ask the learners to suggest what would be a good way for them to practise it, making their own suggestions and negotiating with the teacher the instructions to be followed in the activity.

4 Bearing in mind the difficulty some children may have in refraining from getting the 'right' answer immediately by measuring rather than estimating first, it would be good to ensure that they did predict by using the estimates for something other than just checking the measurements. One obvious such activity would be to see if any improvement occurred in the accuracy of the estimates over the duration of the activity, whether they were better at certain kinds of estimating (larger units), or what the mean variation was. Such activities would also improve the learning of the purpose of estimation by focussing attention on the difference between the estimated and the measured values.

What we have done so far, then, is to diagnose what happened in the incident, interpreting it by comparing what theory seemed to be in use to certain principles of social justice, in order to work out a new strategy according to those principles. It should be clear from this that socially critical research is intensely practical.

WIDER SOCIAL IMPLICATIONS

Thus far, however, we have been concentrating more upon the particular situation than upon the wider social issues. It is in contextualising this incident and generalising from it that our analysis becomes more traditionally academic and societal. Moving on to a more general analysis then, one finds that this incident illustrates an aspect of classroom meta-learning that has broad social implications: the teacher actually wanted the children to do something that they would never do in other spheres of life as a preparation for those other spheres of life.[8] In effect, they were not being asked to predict, but to practise prediction and measurement, which is a very different thing, especially in terms of the context in which it occurs. Evidence for this is the fact that some of them were crossing out their predictions after obtaining measurements, just as one would in a situation in which they would measure for some purpose other than mere practice. So it seems that the children were actually predicting and measuring rather than merely practising because they did not know that their teacher wanted them just to practise. So here is another contradiction: the children were seen to be doing 'the wrong thing' in using in school the operation as they would use it in life outside school.

It is only in school learning that one frequently does this kind of thing, and it is done in spite of the constant complaints in many sections of the media and the community that school is too divorced from other spheres of life. But there are actually very good reasons for doing so. Taking this incident to illustrate the point, few people would argue either that it is not a 'good thing' for children to be able to measure and estimate and use estimates to check measurements, or that all children would learn these things equally well outside school. The activity was therefore a useful and legitimate one; but the way in which the processes of school learning the children were supposed to follow were not clearly and explicitly explained to them, is quite the opposite. What they really lacked was not more easily understood procedural instructions, but an understandable explanation, not just of what estimation is for, how it is done in other spheres of life, and how and why they are doing it in school, but how and why these two differ. So principles of social justice would not only require the use of a different strategy for the original learning, but would also require the learning of different things. By seeing this incident as typical of schooling and illustrative of an aspect of the school–community relation, we have located this incident in the wider social context.

Another more general socially critical aspect comes from asking why it was that this obviously diligent and well intentioned teacher did not herself see the contradictions implicit in her practice. Apart from the fact that she had never been shown how to do the kind of analysis necessary, the answer is that it is not so much that there were contradictions in this particular teacher's practice as that there are contradictions in the 'good' practices teachers have been taught and are expected to use. The contradiction that in order to perform the activity children already needed to know the very thing they were supposed to learn through performing the activity, is inherent in an approach to mathematics teaching in which the children are supposed to 'discover' things that have been set by a predetermined syllabus. When teachers refrain from telling students so that they can find it out for themselves, the contradiction noted in this incident is inevitable.

And this raises another important feature of socially critical analysis: an assumption is made that the actions of individuals are always an intelligent response to more general social determinations. Individual people are seen to be in a contradictory position in which they are often both autonomous actors and unwilling or unwitting 'agents' of ideas inscribed in practices. If we accept this view then we cannot place responsibility for the difficulty experienced by the children in this lesson wholly on the individual teacher: we also have to locate responsibility on the system that has constructed the practices this teacher employed and which has also been primarily responsible for the construction of her view of those practices.

It is in theorising such general phenomena and explaining why the specific practical changes suggested are necessary, that one moves between micro- and macro-analysis in socially critical research. In other words, socially critical analysis operates at and between both the particularities of this particular teacher's particular observations of the particular activity in this particular classroom with these particular children on this particular day, and the broadly social and political questions of how schools operate and why.

Although I have not been able to provide very detailed answers to those more general questions, it is reasonably clear that teachers teach in particular ways for two major reasons: they have been taught that that is how they should teach, and they are so constrained by their conditions of employment that they have little alternative. Teachers' professional practice is said to be over-determined, which means that there are a number of different factors each of which would be sufficient to produce the same result, and which therefore do so all the more completely together.

For example, in this instance it is not just a matter of making teachers use strategies which are inherently contradictory and unjust in some ways, but also of constraining democratic practices by giving teachers so many learners at once that the children are rendered communicatively incompetent, as well as by asking teachers to teach more than can be enjoyably and effectively learned by all in the time allowed (as the standard 50 per cent pass mark indicates), and so on. Such factors thus combine to place teachers in a situation in which they are largely forced simply to decide what the children will do, and then to ensure to the best of the limited resources at their disposal that they do it. This classroom situation is reinforced by other systems, such as the way in which the majority of classroom contextualised pre- and in-service education of teachers is concerned with questions of managing the implementation of the set syllabus rather than issues of social justice.

And so that brings us to a final feature of a socially critical analysis: how things are is never seen as having occurred by chance and for no particular reason; all social systems and their practices are seen to be as they are in order to serve the interests of particular groups. More than any other large professional group, teachers must be controlled, for they are best placed to change society by changing the habits of and instilling ideas in future citizens. If teachers were taught and given the time to analyse their teaching in the way and from the point of view that I have done here, they would not only replace most so-called teacher educators and 'educational' researchers, but they would also demand quite different working conditions and rewards. But should that not, after all, be the expected outcome of effective socially critical analysis?

CONCLUSION

In creating a critical incident with wide social implications from an episode that appeared to be a minor practical managerial matter, I have tried to show that analysis is not a value-neutral process which reveals 'the values' inherent in an incident; on the contrary, as current deconstructive approaches have shown so clearly, the values that are revealed by analysis tend to depend both upon the analysis and on what values we think ought to be present.

Every practice has social implications which should be consonant with our values, and the incident in this chapter shows how even the simplest way of organising a classroom activity embodies value judgements which will be passed on to those who participate. Because children learn about themselves and school learning from our teaching practices, it is imperative to informed professional judgement that we recognise and understand the values we teach so that we can rationally choose those that we wish to espouse and develop, and those which we wish to minimise, counter and avoid.

That involves comparison and contrast, two basic and powerful forms of analysis. But it is only when we have articulated our values and desires that we can compare these with those of our practices. Unfortunately, teachers are usually only required to lay out and critique their values in university philosophy courses, usually in initial preparation, where, because of a lack of understanding of an connection to their practice, the activity tends to be dismissed as yet another example of the 'airy-fairy' uselessness of academic education.

A third major point of this chapter has been that critical incident analysis produces more than just scholarly academic knowledge. When the analysis is of real incidents in actual classroom practice, the understanding gained implies action. In contrast to the kind of theory–practice dichotomy that so often characterises the (non-)relation of research to teaching, one can see here how the practical outcomes depend entirely upon the 'theoretical' values analysis.

Finally, although I have concentrated on social processes and outcomes in this chapter, I have also shown how all the other kinds of analysis first mentioned in Chapter 2 are necessary for and come together in socially critical analysis. In the next and final chapter I want to show how those forms of analysis produce four different kinds of professional judgement all of which are essential to teaching.

Chapter 9

Critical incidents and professional judgement

Country people are often portrayed as gullible and more easily intimidated by qualified professionals than city people. But when my father, who was a general practitioner, moved from the city to a seaside village, he had rather a different experience. The first patient he treated was a local fisherman. It was a complicated though not a serious ailment. Deciding on the best course of treatment, my father wrote out the prescription. 'If it's not improved by next week, you'd better come to see me again', he said as he handed it to the patient. 'Oh yes', the fisherman replied, 'and how many guesses will you want, doctor?'

INTRODUCTION: PROFESSIONAL JUDGEMENT

People sometimes ask what teachers get from the analysis of critical incidents, to which the broad answer is 'improved professional judgement'. It is a term which I have frequently used without having described in much detail what I mean by it or why I think it so important, so that is the task of this chapter.

Most people think that the difficult thing about being a member of the high-status professions such as law and medicine is mastering large amounts of academically difficult specialist knowledge. But the high value ascribed to members of the professions by society comes more from other aspects of their work. They protect, maintain and improve peoples' physical and material well-being. But so do other occupations. A profession is not much valued for helping others or for the sheer amount of essential expert knowledge that its members have to acquire. Rather, members of a profession are valued for their ability to act in situations where a lack of knowledge (there not being a 'the right answer') demands sound judgement (Schön 1983).

Professional judgement is thus a matter of 'expert guesses' and has more to do with reflection, interpretation, opinion and wisdom, than with the mere acquisition of facts and prescribed 'right answers'. Whether to sue or not, for how much and on what grounds; or precisely what is wrong with a patient and whether to treat the illness with drugs, diet, lifestyle changes, surgery or a combination of all of them, are massively complicated decisions that have enormous impact upon the client's well-being. So, although the vast majority of practice in the high-status professions actually involves the repeated execution of many similarly relatively low-level technical skills, value is produced as much by the judgement of uncertain possibilities as upon certain factual knowledge; and as much upon the importance of the consequences of those choices for the client's well-being as upon the efficient performance of skilled routines.

One of the reasons that teaching is not a high-status profession is that few people realise just how incessantly teachers have to make professional judgements, nor do they recognise the tremendous impact those judgements have upon the well-being of students. The strong tradition of technical approaches to 'teacher development' show just how few people realise how teaching is characterised by the need to determine courses of action in situations where knowledge is too limited for there to be a single or obvious 'right answer'. Put another way, teaching is a very indeterminate practice (Pratte 1986).

To demonstrate this aspect of teaching I shall analyse some more incidents, and in so doing explore the kinds of knowledge that teachers use in some of the judgements that they have to make. The incidents have been chosen to show how the different kinds of professional judgement already suggested (practical, diagnostic, reflective and critical) are all essential to teaching, particularly to the life-long well-being of children.

We shall begin by looking at a teacher using practical judgement to inform her action.

PRACTICAL AND DIAGNOSTIC JUDGEMENT

Laughter occurs surprisingly frequently in most classrooms, and most teachers recognise its importance and power. This is one such teacher.

Incident 52: The whole class laughed

Troy said he was sometimes too scared to sleep in case something bad might happen. The teacher suggested in reply, 'So what do you do? Sleep with your eyes open?' The class laughed at this and the teacher continued, 'Don't laugh, I have an aunty who sleeps with her eyes open!' The class laughed some more and the teacher went on, 'She does! She used to frighten the daylights out of us. We'd take her in a cup of tea in the morning and she'd be lying there staring at nothing (the teacher gave a wide-eyed stare); we thought she was dead!' The class laughed some more, along with the Team Teacher and myself at the back of the room.

(Hall 1989)

This incident occurred with a class of 12–13-year-olds. As an introduction to a story about fear, the children were being asked by the teacher to talk about things that frightened them. The plot may be summarised as follows.

Mistake

(a) Troy spoke of something he feared;
(b) the teacher responded with an apparently absurd suggestion;
(c) the whole class laughed.

Recovery

(d) The teacher told them to stop laughing;
(e) she told them a story about her aunt at which they all laughed.

Laughter is both a joyous unifying experience and also a devastatingly destructive weapon. What makes it one or the other is often a matter of who is laughing at what. So what was being laughed at here?

On the surface, the class were laughing at what the teacher said. But, because she was making a joke out of Troy's contribution, and Troy was talking about himself, it was actually Troy who was being laughed at. The laughter was probably mixed (because when teacher makes a joke, everyone laughs), but the underlying message of the teacher's comment was that Troy's fears, and therefore Troy himself as the owner of those fears, were not to be taken seriously. In that sense, the laughter was a humiliation for Troy.

So the first part of the incident shows an unfair attack on Troy which would not only cause him some distress, but would also discourage other children from making further contributions to the discussion. That must, by any account, have been a fairly serious practical mistake on the part of a teacher.

It is, of course, inevitable that we all make such mistakes occasionally, whether we make them as a teacher, parent, spouse or friend. The difference between most people and a really professional and experienced teacher, however, is that the teacher recognises such mistakes even as they occur, and is able to act swiftly and effectively to undo them before any (more) damage is done to anyone. This is such a teacher, and it is worthwhile examining the incident in some detail so that we can admire the way she recovered the situation.

Having made an inappropriate response, the teacher had to do two things: first she had to stop the class laughing at Troy; and second, she had to transform the incident, so that neither the class nor the boy would read or remember it as an occasion when they all laughed at Troy. The way she achieved the first was by telling them not to laugh at the idea that Troy should sleep with his eyes open; and the second by then deliberately making them all laugh at the idea that someone else did sleep with her eyes open. So the real meaning of her first telling them not to laugh, was not that the class must not laugh – period, but that they had misunderstood her, so that their laughter was inappropriate in some way, and that they must therefore stop laughing at what it was they were laughing at. Without actually explicitly saying so, she had guided them to the only other possibility: that, contrary to their immediate reaction, they were to take Troy's problem seriously.

But because that was contrary to the class's initial reaction, it required some kind of justification. To justify and explain why Troy's comment was to be taken seriously, she made out that what they had taken to be a laughable suggestion could in fact be perfectly reasonable. Superficially, that was achieved by the story of her aunt. But the story also achieved much more than that. First, it effectively put Troy onto an equal footing with her aunt, and therefore not only in a close relationship to herself, but in a relationship where Troy had the higher status (Troy = aunt; teacher = niece ∴ aunt → niece = Troy → teacher). That alone was an elevation which more than recompensed Troy for his momentary humiliation. Second, because the story was about an unknown and unelaborated (and therefore archetypical) aunt, the laughter was changed from, 'we laugh at one of us' to 'we laugh at one of them'. It is very difficult to instantly stop a whole class laughing at something they find genuinely funny; it is far more effective to deflect it, covering the move with other laughter. But, third, her story did more than simply deflect the laughter of the class from Troy: it transformed it from dividing and humiliating laughter to a joyous laughter which reunified them all in shared pleasure again. Under such expert professional guidance, the class continued smoothly on its way.

Finally, a couple of more general points about the incident may be worth making with regard to the professional responsibilities and practical skills of teachers. First, it is a good example of the way in which behaviour and values are continuously taught in classrooms. Here the teacher was implicitly (but nevertheless actively) teaching two messages: first, that it was alright to laugh at the same thing in certain circumstances, but not in others; and second, that who was being laughed at by whom was crucial in determining whether it was appropriate (personally and socially acceptable) or not. How teachers deal with such issues, and thereby shape children's views of themselves and the world, do not reduce to simple facts or routines, but ought surely to be matters for the exercise of professional judgement.

Second, and with regard to the practical skills displayed by this teacher, note that the story of the aunt did not employ logical argument to undo the potential for damage. Troy said he was 'too scared to sleep in case something bad might happen', but the teacher's suggestion that he keep his eyes open when asleep would not enable him to prevent anything bad happening, for he would still be unconscious. But the point of the story was that the aunt was actually asleep with her eyes open. So the class was encouraged to laugh at the aunt for exactly the same reason that they had been told not to laugh at Troy: because it is peculiar to go to sleep with open eyes. So rather than render their laughter at her original response to Troy inappropriate, on logical grounds it should have reinforced it.

But what else could she do (from within the practice in which she was already located)?[1] She had responded 'wrongly', and could only have 'corrected' it logically with an apology. The problem there was that to make an apology would only make a major issue of the matter, the very thing she wished to avoid. So the teacher chose not to operate through syllogistic reasoning; she used instead the logic of dramatic action. She involved them in a performance, carrying them along with what was actually a distraction. By her action she was able to make the whole class believe that their perfectly normal and quite logical reaction to one aspect of the exchange was inappropriate to another. Thus the net effect of her performance was to transform a possibly harmful initial mistake into an incident more likely to benefit Troy. And it was so well done that it was only under subsequent examination that the incident emerged from the lesson transcript; so well-performed was it, that at the time no one present even registered what the drama of the mistake and recovery really involved. So whilst a teacher's role is never beyond critique (what is it about the teacher that she made that kind of a mistake, and why was it she turned somersaults instead of simply apologising?) it is surely the kind of skilled performance which Shulman had in mind when he referred to the unarticulated 'wisdom of practice' (1987: 11).

I have already suggested that a key characteristic of a profession is that there is more than merely a body of specialist knowledge, though it is still very important. Professional specialist knowledge is scientifically verified and formally trans-mitted to initiates who are certified as having mastered it. There are also various forms of 'internship' in which they are required to successfully apply that knowl-edge in the best interests of their clients. Clearly this teacher is a successful practitioner in terms of her acquired expertise, but in what sense does that expertise meet those criteria? It is difficult to see the scientific basis of her knowledge, how it could be proven or generalised, or in what sense it is academic knowledge that could be transmitted to initiates. Is this not expertise which comes from intuition, experience and 'rightmindedness' rather than scholarly disciplinary knowledge? Certainly it is not obvious that to perform in that manner requires the kind of understanding which the professional practitioner could master either through the use of highly developed academic skills or practical 'competencies'. In fact it is hard to categorise the knowledge used here by this teacher as anything other than tacitly held practical conduct knowledge (Polanyi and Prosch 1975). For such reasons teaching has often been characterised as being more of an art than a science.

There is, of course, nothing wrong with characterising teaching as an art: the problem is that it has been characterised as an art like gardening or cookery, not like the art of surgery, design or money-lending. The reason for this is that the artistry of teaching has not been much documented by researchers, and so is not generally recognised.[2] It is necessary therefore, first to document the kind of practical knowledge displayed by such teachers through performing research of a sufficiently pure and micro-nature on teachers' practical skills. Second it is necess-ary to transform the knowledge into more institutionalised academic knowledge, so that it could be publicly recognised as being different, but of similar status, to the kind of knowledge used in the major professions. And third, teachers need to learn, understand and use that knowledge in planning, implementing and evaluating their practice. In short, teachers need to take an diagnostic approach to teaching, which means that they have to understand what happens in classrooms and why, using that knowledge both to choose what action to take, and to justify and learn from their action and its outcomes.

Recent advances in the study of classrooms and teacher thinking suggest that the production of the necessary knowledge base is already well underway, though few teachers have yet taken up and used that knowledge. It is the fact that this teacher, though she is clearly highly skilled at instantly recognising, analysing and dealing with a potentially damaging situation, cannot explain her practice,[3] which leads me to classify this incident as an example of practical professionalism. It is the difference between recognition and the development of a considered diagnosis. To use interpretation in the manner of the major professions teachers would have to be able to deal with their practice at a discursive level; that is, they would need to be able to perform for themselves the kind of diagnosis illustrated above.

These, then, are two kinds of knowledge and expertise necessary to practice in a profession: the practical is that which is fundamental to expert performance of relatively routine technical tasks, and is primarily acquired through learning from practical experience. It involves noticing a situation and responding appropriately to it, which, commonplace as it sounds, is the basis of professional teaching. Diagnosis is another set of skills and knowledge necessary to understand, explain and be able to justify the practical judgement. It explains the practical action taken, and so is more discursive, academic and theoretical, though they are both forms of interpretation. All good teachers have acquired the former, very few the latter.

Returning to the issue of professionalism, we can categorise this incident as an example of teaching which in some ways is excellent, but professional only in the technical sense of the experienced practitioner doing a better job than an untrained or inexperienced person would. Although such technical expertise is the bulk of work in high-status professional practice, on its own I believe it is an insufficient basis for professional judgement. If teachers are to understand and explain their technical expertise in an informed fashion that will enable them to control, develop and justify their practice, they will also need a more obviously analytic and interpretive approach such as that advocated here.

REFLECTIVE JUDGEMENT

Thus far I have argued that a teacher who can change the nature and direction of students' laughter is acting professionally, but merely in the same sense that the golfer who drives a ball much further and more accurately than a recreational player, or the mechanic who quickly and correctly diagnoses and rectifies a fault in a car engine in a way which drivers of the cars could not do for themselves, are acting professionally. To do so, however, is to miss the important point that, even at this very practical level, the teacher was discharging a moral responsibility in her attempt to care for the feelings of a client. She was also informing that caring with expert knowledge about those feelings, how they would affect learning performance and cultivate attitudes towards self and society. Her practical action thus had far wider and more enduring consequences for her clients than ever could the work of golfers and mechanics.

In teaching, other kinds of professional judgement are also necessary, and there is more to these than carrying out in a professional fashion certain routines acquired through natural aptitude and experience. These kinds of professional judgement are characteristic of the professions, and the difference between doing something professionally and being in a profession lies in the range of choices that must be made about how to achieve a particular end, and the importance of the service offered to a client's well-being. The consequences for the well-being of the clients of how well things are done are very much more serious in a profession than in most other occupations. Also, in the professions there is a great deal of choice about how to achieve the clearly stated ends, and in teaching there is also a wide choice of ends. Very little judgement about what is best for the client enters into getting a car engine running well; failure to do so will cause little more than annoyance, and matters can always be corrected in a later attempt. Further, there are only about a dozen things that cause loss of power or difficulty in starting a car, for instance, and there is no choice about how best to do it: the mechanic follows a diagnostic algorithm to find and correct the fault. Little interpretation and judgement are required: if the points are burnt, they must be replaced. Similarly in teaching, very little interpretation or judgement enters into whether or not to silence a class of students so that they can listen to the teacher, and, as we have seen, it is a relatively easy matter for a skilled practitioner to achieve. Just one kind of professional judgement is necessary when a definite answer is known for a certain problem.

But situations often arise in teaching for which there is no known appropriate course of action, let alone an approved solution which can simply be recalled from a stock of professional knowledge. And rather than being the exception, as they are in general medicine, these situations are the norm in classroom teaching. As almost every incident has demonstrated, in teaching many decisions are not simple matters in which the teacher can identify a situation and recall and apply the correct course of action. And as in law and medicine, the judgements teachers have to make concern the well-being of their students, so are not merely epistemological, but also ethical decisions Lyons (1990). Contrary to law and medicine, however, teaching judgements cannot be made on an individual basis: every dealing a teacher has with one student will affect the other students in the class in one way or another, which vastly increases the complexity and stress of the situation. This next incident is about just such a dilemma: when a student misbehaves, how does one judge who should suffer and in what way? It illustrates how thinking teachers exercise much the same kind of judgement as do lawyers and doctors, but they do so with a specifically moral orientation. Because it was such a dramatic incident there was no difficulty in recognising the problems with the outcome. Although the teacher was not diagnosing the matter, she was thinking in a reflective fashion that involved judging the effects of her action and weighing up (future) alternative strategies. This process suggests a third kind of interpretation, personal reflection:

Incident 53: Spitting

A secondary science teacher in one of my groups told us how, when she asked a class to line up outside the laboratory before a lesson, one boy at the front of the line, a notorious trouble-maker, spat 'a great gob of slime' at her feet. 'If you want to clear your throat' she said, 'it is usual to use a hanky.' Everyone laughed. 'OK. In you go,' she said, and they all filed in. The boy who spat then spent the whole lesson writing over and over again in his science book, 'I hate (name of the) school'. The teacher ignored him, quite pleased that he was keeping to himself and not needing further discipline. During recess, however, he was involved in a serious fight, and had to be suspended from the school. The teacher then felt she was partly responsible. On the one hand she felt she had quietly and effectively controlled the boy in a way that only capable and experienced teachers are so effortlessly able to do, but on the other she felt that the effect of her having done so had led the boy to seek some other outlet for his fury.

There are a number of dilemmas here that are of the same order with regard to the client's well-being as are found in the major professions. The one which really bothered this teacher (and which her reflective skills had led her to articulate) was whether she should have accepted his challenge, thus dealing with him much less effectively with regard to her discipline, but meeting at not inconsiderable personal expense his need to be seen as an effective troublemaker. As she put it,

> If I'd said to him, 'How dare you spit at me? Stand outside until I can take you straight to the deputy principal', would he still be at the school? And if he were, how would I deal with him next time, how would the others' learning suffer from the constant interruptions, and might others follow his lead more easily?[4]

It is the nature of teaching that one has to act instantly and ask such questions afterwards (which is why judgement of the instant and practical kind is so important), and it is also the nature of teaching that there are no correct answers to such questions: they are always matters of professional judgement. A more discursive and overtly 'academic' diagnostic analysis of this incident can achieve two purposes, however: first, it demonstrates the complex, stressful and problematic nature of teaching, which is a vital first step towards public recognition of the professional nature of teaching. And second, it provides the teacher with a better understanding of the 'how' and 'why' of what happened. This is necessary for two aspects of professional development. First, a diagnostic understanding would have enabled this teacher to learn from her professional practice and thereby increase her control over it; second, any moral deliberation that might have occurred, would depend upon a sound diagnosis of the incident.

So what did happen? First, it was clear that the teacher had in fact administered a massive put-down to the boy when he spat. Spitting is perhaps the most abusive form of challenge the boy could offer her, but she had simply pretended to read the action publicly as evidence of the unmannerly and ignorant qualities of the challenger. Spitting must always be dealt with because it is never tolerated; but coughing, sneezing, throat-clearing and even flatulence often pass entirely unnoticed, or they occasionally merit a mild and often humorous reproach. In reading so aberrantly the boy's spitting as a throat-clearing, the teacher was stating that she could not accept that the boy spat at her because there was no way in which he could seriously challenge her. Denying that he spat denied his ability to challenge her. The boy, expecting to be dealt with for spitting at a teacher, was too taken aback to respond. Capitalising on the laughter to move the class into the laboratory and thus terminating the exchange, the teacher then took away any opportunity the boy might have had to mount another challenge.

In one sense, the teacher had thus very adroitly dealt with the challenge, not by ignoring it, but by pretending there was no challenge. At the most practical level, this was done 'professionally', but it produced serious problems with regard to the well-being of the student.

In my analysis[5] she had downgraded the boy in at least four important aspects of his self-esteem. First, she had proved him to be so socially backward that he had not yet learned the basic manners of how people managed their bodily fluids in public; second and consequently, she had shown him to be so low in status that when he issued a challenge it would not be recognised as such; third, he had failed to make trouble for the teacher, but instead brought it upon himself, so he was not even successful in ways that he and everyone else always expected him to be. Finally, for a black, authority defeating, chauvinistic young male, all this had been quickly and effortlessly done to him by a white, middle-aged, middle-class woman.

This teacher was operating at a level of concern that is well beyond the purely practical. In contrast to the previous teacher, she made an interpretation of the nature and effects of her actions that questioned her judgement and habitual practice. It was not simply a matter of registering the fact that her action had upset the boy, but of reflecting upon the priorities she had assigned in the incident, and, in a more general sense, the professional values she had espoused and which therefore led her to do certain things in particular ways. So although she did not have the level of expertise necessary to analyse it in the same detail that I did, her recognition of the dilemma did not depend on that analysis, though any subsequent moral deliberation of the particular incident would have. Overall, then, this is an example of professional judgement quite different from anything encountered in golf or motor mechanics, and probably more difficult (in the sense that there is less proven knowledge about it) than many of the more difficult situations in medicine or law. The ability to identify and reflect upon such situations therefore represents a third kind of interpretation, one which is found in all the major professions, but which is actually more frequent and complex in teaching. This I will term 'reflective' interpretation, and, to be a professional characteristic, it would have to be practised through expertise in moral deliberation of the kind Tom (1984) and Lister and Zeichner (1987) for instance, have advocated.

THE IMPORTANCE OF SIDE-EFFECTS

Throughout this book I have stressed the importance of teaching decisions, and the last example indicated just how far-reaching the effects of a single utterance from a teacher can be. Unfortunately for teachers, the outcomes of teaching are very seldom so obvious and immediate, but are almost invariably very diffuse and long-term affairs. Whereas one sees the results of law and medicine immediately and experiences them obviously and directly (people get better or avoid jail), the main effects of teaching are often produced by the hidden curriculum, and as such would be classified as 'side-effects' in medicine. Furthermore the majority of teaching decisions are especially invisible to the clients at the time. The next example is included to show the importance of teachers having the expert knowledge to be able to work at the necessarily high level demanded. It is an extract from part of an interview with an intelligent 11-year-old girl.

Incident 54: Place value

We were going over Katie's weekly test in which the following was written:

14. $\underline{4}$.96	=	P	1s	M	4s	✓
15. 187$\underline{2}$6	=	P	100ths	M	200ths	✓
16. 3$\underline{7}$6.275	=	P	10s	M	7s	X

I: What do the P and M stand for?

K: The P's the place, and the M's ... I don't know, I think it means how much or something.

I: (*Pointing to Question 15*) What does the 200ths mean then?

K: It's two hundredths.

I: Do you mean it's two one-hundredths, or one two-hundredths?

K: It's two hundredths.

I: We'll have to work on that.

* * *

I: (*Pointing to Question 16*) Why was the 7s marked wrong?

K: It should have been seventies.

L: Why is that?

K: Because it's seventies.

I: So what's this 's' bit?

K: That's how we do them.

I: But what does it mean?

K: I don't know.

I: Shouldn't it have been 70?

K: Look, leave me alone will you? That's how we do them, and I usually get them right, don't I?

I have included this exchange because it illustrates the difficulty of diagnosis and the importance of setting similar standards for teaching as are current for practice in the major professions. With regard to the first aspect, if one goes by the test results, as most parents, teachers and administrators do, then this child is doing well because she did indeed get the correct answer to 95 per cent of the questions. So any general reflection on this would be more likely to conclude with a congratulation than with further inquiry. It is for that reason that diagnosis prior to reflection is so important. Analysis of my interview shows that she is neither learning much mathematics, nor developing an interest in understanding it. She is instead learning how to get the right answers, which is a very different thing.

The cause for concern is not that Katie does not understand the hundredth/two hundredth or the seventy/seventies distinctions, for those will indeed come in time; the problem is the side effect of her lack of understanding. She has learned two things: first, that in order to do well in mathematics it is not necessary to think about or to try to understand what one is required to do; and second, all that matters is 'getting it right', even if it does not even make sense. As these are hardly what the teacher or anyone else intended her to learn, they are side-effects of the way in which she has been taught. This particular child had ambitions to be a vet. To do that she would need to study mathematics to a fairly high level. It would not be likely that she would make it from her current understanding. Is this not as serious an effect on a person's life as a chronic ailment or law suit?

Most people think that the worst result of poor teaching is merely a failure to learn something at a particular time. But the important and generally totally unrecognised point demonstrated here, is that children do not simply fail to learn something: every time learning or 'not learning' occurs, they learn something about learning or not learning. Children who fail to learn something often learn from that failure that they cannot learn that thing, an experience which is often compounded into learning that they cannot learn, period. Again, professional judgement in teaching is more difficult in this respect than in medicine where a failure to cure does not always aggravate the disease; more often it simply leaves it unchanged.

So what children learn about learning in school is of great consequence to both the individual and society. In this case, for instance, there is currently great concern about the lack of mathematicians, and consequently of maths teachers. Yet here we have a child who has been taught by six different teachers, none of whom had a mathematical background themselves, but who need to be able to communicate to students understandings and attitudes towards the subject which they themselves do not have.

In view of my concern with the poor image that teaching is given by the media and others working in education, it is unfortunate that the example illustrates a negative side-effect, but, as is so often the case, we are much better able to recognise when something has gone wrong than we are able to see that it is going or might go wrong. Therefore the question is, just how do children come to learn such things as that mathematics is a matter of correct recall and not understanding? For many such side-effects the answer is that we simply do not know, for very little of that kind of research has yet been done. Occasionally, however, we discover an incident in which the processes involved are very explicit, and shortly after the above incident I was working with a teacher who had discovered through diagnosing an incident that he was inadvertently communicating just such messages about mathematics to his class.

In this case the incident was unintentionally reported to me by a teacher during a university course for in-service teachers. The teacher, John, was concerned about the behaviour of Chris, a 12-year-old boy in his class. John had found Chris very annoying in various ways, and thought he was underachieving. John had been observing Chris's behaviour in order to plan some kind of an intervention, and he was now reporting a 'typical' exchange. The following account is a shortened version of what John had written in his critical incident research file:

Incident 55: Fractions

I began the day by marking the maths homework which was five division of fractions problems of the kind: $\frac{3}{5} \div \frac{3}{10}$. My method was to ask one student for the answer, and then go through it on the board.

$\frac{3}{5} \div \frac{3}{10}$

'You write down $\frac{3}{5}$, then there are three steps to solving the problem. First you change the sign (i.e. $\frac{3}{5} \times \frac{3}{10}$).

Then you inverse [sic] (or turn up the other way) the second fraction (i.e. $\frac{3}{5} \times \frac{10}{3}$.

The third step is to see if you can cancel. Always try to cancel the biggest numbers first (i.e. $\frac{3}{5} \times \frac{10}{3}$ then, $\frac{3}{1} \times \frac{2}{3}$).

Now multiply out across on both sides of the fraction (i.e. $\frac{3}{1} \times \frac{2}{3} = \frac{6}{3} = \frac{2}{1} = 2$). Who got that? Good! Now the others are done exactly the same.'

After doing them all and explaining the three major steps in each, I turned to the class and asked in a very quiet concerned tone: 'Now, does anyone not understand any of these three steps?'

Chris, who I'd identified as lacking confidence in his own abilities and who I later decided is hampered by his poor concentration (he doesn't listen closely to instructions) – put his hand up and said: 'I don't understand what you do there', and pointed to the first step of changing the sign. Then I hit the roof. 'Well it's no wonder you don't understand, because you don't listen! This is the first of three easy steps.' Then, turning to the class, I said. 'This boy has a problem. He doesn't listen. It's not that he can't learn. It's that he won't listen and that stops him from learning.' I then got from the class the steps of solving these problems and went through the last five asking Chris what to do next. He was able to tell me each step without much hesitation. I congratulated him then and reminded him of the need to listen and concentrate – 'That's how you learn'.

As gently as I could, I pointed out what I thought might be happening. No child could have 'understood' the first step because John had simply repeated an algorithm for memorisation, which did not explain anything and even that was confusing because the three steps' were presented as four. John wasn't sure whether Chris could do the sums or not, but that is not the point: John conflated knowing to change the sign with understanding why it is that one does it, and gave the whole class a very important lesson on the greater importance of the former. So here was an example of the kind of process that had probably formed Katie's attitudes to mathematics revealed by the previous incident. John's students were not only learning how to do the division of fractions; they were learning that mathematics is something you should memorise rather than try to understand, and furthermore, that you should always pretend to have understood it. The incident explained something about why Chris might be under-achieving.

As we talked around the problem, John reflected upon why the incident had occurred:

Incident 56: Maths memory

I thought back further to my high school mathematics classes, and from Year 9 onwards this was the reason I did not do well. I was always looking for a formula to solve the problems, rather than understanding what the problem meant and what was actually happening to the numbers and why. And here I am, more than 15 years later trying to get my Grade 6 students to 'remember 3 easy steps' and not to consider the 'why' of mathematics. It never occurred to me to show them 'why' the problems are done in these 3 steps. I've yet to work that out for myself. How guilty I feel. It wasn't even laziness, just sheer lack of understanding and foresight on my behalf.

Tomorrow I am spending the time until recess on mathematics, having children working in groups to discuss and work out the 'why' for these fraction problems.

Having seen and accepted the implications of what he had done, John was changing his teaching in order to overcome the problem. If he had not been a dedicated teacher, he would not have been attending the course in his own time and at his own expense, let alone willingly suffering such challenges to his professional self-esteem. John is known to be a very good teacher, but when I showed the account of the original incident (anonymously) to four people who, in different ways, were responsible for John's teaching, all but one (who made no comment) blamed John, as indeed he himself did. In a very real sense, however, such teaching has very little to do with the actual teacher, but is caused by other people, elsewhere. In Australia at any rate, most primary school teachers will not have studied mathematics beyond the minimum school-leaving age, and they will have been given less than one hundred hours' preparation for teaching the subject by their tertiary institution which will, however, certify them to teach it for life. Then, as in this case, the teachers' employers will have done nothing to further educate them either in terms of their own understanding of mathematics or in how best to teach it. Both groups will, however, happily blame John for failing to understand things that they have effectively prevented him from learning.[6]

Returning to the main theme, then, these last examples demonstrate two important points: first they provide instances of the kind of problems that arise when the previous two types of practice-to-knowledge relationship are absent. Detailed diagnosis of the phenomena was not occurring, and because nothing in the normal teaching–learning process overtly indicated that some kind of reflection was required, the practice did not become a matter for professional judgement, and the effects for the clients and society were not recognised. Second, teachers are not solely to blame: given the kind and amount of professional training that most teachers have had, to expect the outcomes of their mathematics teaching to be anything other than a reproduction of their own school experience, is absurd. It is quite unrealistic to expect them to either know about the problem or to be able to recognise it. The teachers are but the last in a line of responsibility, and their very lack of opportunity to know more about the matter makes them the least culpable.

CRITICAL JUDGEMENT

Thus far I have illustrated three kinds of professional judgement in teaching. The first is an instant and practical kind by which experienced and skillful teachers make the majority of their teaching decisions. The second, diagnosis, produces an explanation of the first, and leads to a conscious understanding of the nature and effects of the practical decisions made. These first two I have termed practical judgement for doing and diagnostic judgement for understanding. The outcome of the third kind of judgement, termed 'reflective', is rather different, however. It involves a more subjective evaluation of the incident and is most common when the teacher knows there are no obvious 'right answers' about to how to act. I have suggested that all teachers who learn from experience become expert at practical judgement; that those who are also concerned and feeling people naturally reflect; but that very few teachers perform the kind of analysis necessary for a diagnostic judgement.

I now want to move on to a fourth kind of professional judgement which involves both a reflective critical attitude and the gathering of diagnostic information about professional practices through more formal and interventional research strategies. It is well-illustrated in the following example which is based upon an extract from a teacher's professional critical incident research file. The teacher is beginning action research on tale-telling.

Incident 57: Tale-telling

(*In my class*) Eleven boys and five girls were today's 'tale-tellers' ... I noticed that by far the most children approached me. The aide had one interaction and the school experience student two.

Why? Are the children already so aware of authority figures? Do they perceive the different role of a teacher from an aide? ... Does the same child come to all three of us, or do certain children find it easier to interact with certain adults? If a child does go to all three of us, why? ... Is it just attention seeking, or are there other causal factors?

The person writing was a very competent and experienced primary school teacher. Tale-telling was not something she was overly concerned about, but had simply accepted as a normal feature of classroom interaction with children at that age. But the entry demonstrates teacher professionalism, in a number of ways. First, that she wondered about the nature and function of tale-telling in class at all was the result of further professional study, which meant that she was not simply repeating the same strategies year after year, but was constantly seeking to update and improve her professional knowledge. Second, she could look seriously at such a relatively minor aspect of her teaching only because all the more important things were already being handled extremely well; she was at the stage of polishing her performance. Third, she was not basing judgements on casual impressions and intuitions, but had methodically set about collecting data on the phenomenon that she was dealing with. And fourth, she formed a number of specific hypotheses from the data which she could use to direct further investigation. So overall the entry shows her approach to be dedicated and scientific, both of which are important features of doing a skilled job professionally.

This teacher's critical incidents also demonstrate a level of professionalism considerably beyond the practical. First, although certain kinds of frequencies of tale-telling may cause annoyance, it is by no means clear that tale-telling is a problem as such: it may just be an integral and necessary part of social development which, like children's addiction to cartoons at certain ages, is normally grown through to more adult behaviour. Whether it is a problem or not depends almost entirely upon one's knowledge of social development and conception of acceptable behaviour. Whether one knows something or not is the result of a skilling process; but judgements about socially acceptable behaviour are a matter of a teacher's professional value system, and the 'correctness' of the choices they are led to make about what action to take will be judged according to that system, and not according to any purely technical standards about what might be a single 'right answer'. In terms of the complexity and necessity for judgement, then, the matter this teacher is dealing with is much more like a legal or medical problem than a mechanical one.

Second, it is also a professional matter in terms of the consequences for the clients. I pointed out that more boys than girls seemed to be telling tales. She wondered what had happened because it was usually the girls who told more tales. She collected more data and then wrote:

Incident 58: Boys' gossip

I was actually surprised to find that the boys were the main tale tellers. I mentioned it to the aide that, 'One day sixteen children told tales, and fifteen of them were ...', and she filled in, 'girls', for me. That made me wonder if other people thought that girls told more tales than boys, like I used to. So I spoke about my findings to five other colleagues and my husband, and everyone assumed that it was the girls who were the tale tellers ... (Gender-based) negative assumptions and expectations are made of both sexes. Not until the conditioning (that results from these assumptions) is dispelled, will each person be able to function to their full human potential (and be) equally acceptable.

Here we can see that the matter is not simply a relatively minor technical aspect of interaction management within a classroom, but is integral with the broader context of the social construction of gender roles and expectations which will have great influence throughout her students' lives.

Tale-telling is considered by most people to be childish and unnecessary. But it is in fact quite a complicated functional process, and cannot be dismissed merely as the unnecessary bothering of public authority with trivial private concerns. Tale-telling is used competitively to gain individual advantage over peers, both by drawing attention to the shortcomings of others, and by demonstrating the extent of the tale-teller's compliance to the authority. That boys told more tales than girls in that class, suggests that there was more competition amongst the boys; but more important, the adults' perception that girls told more tales is a gendered judgement: girls tell tales, but boys report incidents. Such judgements about children mature into judgements about adults, such as that women gossip but men discuss. So two important factors can be seen here: one, if gossip and tale-telling are disapproved, so girls' discussions and reports, because they are labelled gossip and tale-telling, will be disapproved; and two, we know that people tend to do what others expect of them, so girls will feel that it's alright for them to engage in behaviour that will be labeled gossip and tale-telling. The longer term outcomes are obvious: if girls learn to see themselves as people who gossip and tell tales rather than as people who discuss and report, then they will tend to do the former rather than the latter, thus developing quite the wrong skills, attitudes and self-images for the competitive world of the workplace. So what is actually happening here is that girls are being taught to perform according to a gendered label. In this matter, then, the consequences are again of a kind more akin to the effects of legal and medical practice than of more purely technical jobs.

Flowing from the last point, this incident reveals the nature of professional judgement in teaching in a deeper way. Even when this teacher appears to merely follow a technical routine, she recognises how it is actually herself, as one who acts upon her own personal attitudes, beliefs and expectations in her classroom, who cultivates the attitudes and expectations that have such far-reaching consequences for the students. She is prepared for self-criticism of a kind which reaches right into her consciousness, a very different process from the kind of quality control expected of other than professional occupations. Furthermore, in writing a professional critical incident research file to document, explore and question her action

and values, she is being professional in her critique of her professional consciousness and judgements.

CONCLUSION

To summarise the substantive issue of this chapter, I have suggested that four kinds
of judgement are necessary to professional teaching.

1   *Practical judgement* which is the basis of every action taken in the conduct of
teaching, and the majority of which is made instantly.
2   *Diagnostic judgement* which involves using profession-specific knowledge
and academic expertise to recognise, describe, understand and explain and
interpret practical judgements.
3   *Reflective judgement* which concerns more personal and moral judgements
involving the identification, description, exploration and justification of the
judgements made and values implicit and espoused in practical (teaching)
decisions and their explanations.
4   *Critical judgement*, which, through formal investigation, involves challenge to
and evaluation of the judgements and values revealed by reflection.

Contrary to the logic of the way in which I have presented them, personal
experience suggests that these kinds of judgement are not necessarily successively
dependent, though I think they ought to be. The majority of teachers I have
encountered who do think about their practice, do not work much, if at all, through
analysis, especially diagnosis; rather they tend to make practical and reflective
judgements. It would seem important, however, that each kind of judgement should
be deployed upon the judgement produced by the previous form; in particular, the
outcomes of reflection on practice greatly depend upon how the practice is
explained and interpreted. So it seems to me that these forms should be sequentially
employed.

This must not be taken to mean that these kinds of judgement are hierarchical
in terms of their importance. Although critical judgement may, in some senses, be
regarded as a further professional activity to practical, it is also the antithesis of
experience and routine, and as such it inhibits the normal transactions essential to
effective teaching. One can become too critically minded to be of any practical use.
Mastery and use of the methods of analysis for all four kinds of judgement are
therefore essential to professional teaching.

Because I am more concerned in this chapter to open up realistic possibilities
for the future of teaching than I am to merely describe the nature of judgements in
teaching and to theorise the idea of professionalism, it is necessary to raise two
important questions. I have suggested that, though most teachers expertly make
practical judgements and are frequently reflective, they generally are not able to
make either diagnostic or critical judgements. So first, do teachers really require
the ability to employ all four kinds of judgement? And second, if they do, how can
teachers develop those aspects of the professionalism of their practice? I have tried

to answer the first in this chapter by showing how an adherence to practical judgement (and/or the inability to use any other) leads (in very subtle ways) to a serious lack of provision for children's (and hence society's) longer-term well-being. The answer to the second of these questions is fortunately the topic of a huge literature and the subject of several important national inquiries, but it appears to me that in the first instance responsibility lies with the academics who teach teachers and perform educational research.

The point is that if the specific examples and general theory of professional judgement that I have outlined are only partially correct, then some things must have prevented teachers from developing them and being regarded as members of an autonomous major profession. The problem is, I think, historical. The way in which education has been institutionalised in universities has created a divided profession. Differences between the agendas of teachers and educational re-searchers had led to the production of knowledge that is not only of more use to those who control teachers than to teachers themselves, but has also reflected teachers badly. How this has come about and what might be done about it are pressing questions which are dealt with in the next chapter, the Conclusion. In this chapter I hope to have shown how the analysis of critical incidents can be used to demonstrate three key aspects of teacher professionalism: (a) the kind of professional skills and knowledge currently possessed by teachers; (b) the kind of skills and knowledge that they need to acquire; and (c) the importance of the consequences of teachers' professional judgements for the lifelong well-being of children.

Conclusion

In this book I have critical incidents to show that basic practical competencies are a necessary but not sufficient condition for a professional approach to teaching. In the previous chapter I argued that quality in teaching lies in teachers' ability to recognise the need for professional judgement and the kind of judgements they make. And in outlining that theory of professionalism I stressed that the judgements teachers make come more from their understanding of the situation and who they are than from any set of teaching procedures that they may follow. I did not much deal with what I meant by 'who we are', so here I want to go on to show that what professional judgements we make depends on the interaction of two aspects of being a teacher: who we are as private people, and who we are as trained and experienced teachers. On the one had we each have an individual and unique set of experiences, interests, values, circumstances and such, that go to make us the kind of person we are; and on the other we subscribe in various ways and to certain degrees to a common set of professional norms that make us the kind of teacher we are.

At a time when teachers are being more rigorously assessed on ever narrower observable criteria, who we are and what we know come to assume a new importance. Who we are as a person will produce quite different outcomes from what appears at first to be the same teaching technique, such as 'rewarding with verbal praise'. And differences in what we know about teaching will make us into different teachers who will make quite different judgements about the same things. One can imagine serious conflict occurring when teachers are told that there is one best way to organise a class, for instance. It may not fit with their professional experience, but they will have to comply if they cannot articulate a critique and defend an alternative. One of the best ways of justifying and explaining practice that is open to teachers is through anecdote: carefully observed and analysed critical incidents can communicate their aims and achievements better than many other kinds of evaluation. Let us now look at how critical incidents can enable us to understand how our personal views and experiences influence our teaching; and why it is important for teachers to begin to develop their own theories of their work.

THE IMPORTANCE OF WHO WE ARE

I began this book with a contrast between a novice and an experienced teacher, making the point that the latter was professionally competent in a way that the former was not. I would like to conclude with another contrast, this time between two equally competent teachers who were achieving different outcomes because of who they were. It is a brief account of a kind of double facilitation: I was supervising the higher degree work of Jeff, a Deputy Principal, who was facilitating the professional development of two teachers new to his school. One was just beginning her second year of teaching, the other her sixth. Both were thoughtful, well-organised and conscientious teachers. The school was in a remote outback mining town and so included a number of Aboriginal students from the surrounding bush. The more experienced teacher had taught Aboriginal children in a similar context for the past five years.

Part of the role of the Deputy Principal in a Western Australian primary school is to keep the roll and chase up absentees. In doing this duty Jeff noticed that one teacher's class consistently had a higher aboriginal absentee rate than the other. Jeff had observed both teachers' classes on a number of occasions, and occasionally taught them. He thought he could detect a 'difference in feeling' between the two, and he preferred the climate of the low absentee class. But he was not aware of anything specific that would explain the differences, so he asked the teachers what they thought was causing the absences of the Aborigines in their classes. Every reason produced by both teachers had to do with the children's home backgrounds; neither mentioned anything about what happened to them in school.

Jeff decided to record some incidents in both classes. The first thing he noticed in the high absentee class was that a succession of questions was directed towards a single group of students which, it turned out, were all (white and) the highest achievers. Comparing this with the low absentee class he found the questions were very widely distributed so that he could detect no colour, ability or gender bias. He also noticed that in the high absentee class the children were for most of the time seated in ability groups, whereas in the low absentee class the children sat in rows all facing the front of the class for their 'desk work', and for discussions and whole class activities the children came to the front and sat on the mat; there were no set groups. He saw that this meant that who was doing well was clearly demonstrated in the high absentee class.

Jeff wondered if this was important and so decided to look at how differences in performance were treated in the classes. As both teachers used verbal praise as reward, he concentrated on this, recording the following exchange between the low absentee class teacher (Lat) and Jake, an Aboriginal child:

Incident 59: Verbal praise 1

Teacher: Oh! What a good effort Jake has put in. He has shown me he is improving. Can you show the class your work Jake, please?

Jake:	Yes Miss L. (*Very proudly shows his work to the whole class*)
Tara:	(*After seeing Jake's work*) I've improved too Miss L!
Teacher:	(*Takes a look at Tara's work*) Yes Tara, you have improved as well. I will be coming round to see all your work and I will be looking for all the people who have improved. Now see if you can improve as you finish off.

Jeff then looked at the high absentee class teacher to see what she did in a similar situation:

Incident 60: Verbal praise 2

Teacher:	(*Speaking loudly to the whole class*) Marcus has done some good work. Isn't it nice to see Marcus trying hard?
	(*The class look up from their work, look at Marcus and continue back with their work.*)
Teacher:	(*A little quieter*) Well Marcus, it's good to see you've tried, but you will have to try harder if you are going to be the best.

Jeff analysed these in some detail, concluding that the differences were that the low absentee class teacher was singling out the child's work as well as the child for approval, and doing so in a way that included everyone in the class. On the other hand, the high absentee class teacher was only singling out the child and doing so in a way that produced a competition which everyone but one must lose. Jeff then followed up these ideas of sharing and competing in his next observations.

Incident 61: Storywriting 1

Morning news. Merline (an Aboriginal child) is asked to tell the group what she did at the week-end. 'Nothing', she replied. The teacher then asked, 'But did you go hunting or out bush with your family?' and Merline shyly replied 'Yes'. 'Well can you tell the class what they shot, what you found to eat?' Merline, seeing that the teacher was interested in her experience began to tell an expansive and detailed account of a highly successful hunting trip that held the attention of the whole class. Merline clearly relished the role of story-teller when she had an appreciative audience, and, exhilarated by the experience wrote some of the story in her diary, showing a general improvement in her work.

Again Jeff found a contrast in the high absentee class:

Incident 62: Storywriting 2

Teacher:	(*To the whole class*) What shall we start our story with? (*Several children call out suggestions*). How shall we start our story? Hands up, please. Yes, Marcia. (*Marcia is an Aboriginal*

> *girl who seldom participates in whole group activities)* It's
> lovely to see your hand up.

Marcia: Bubbles, yeah, bubbles, we made bubbles and they popped.

Teacher: Yes, Marcia, we made bubbles, but how did we start? Hands up
please. Yes Jane. *(A girl from the top group)* All listen to Jane
please.

Jane: We went outside to make bubbles. We took some wire and
some detergent.

(The teacher then wrote Jane's contribution on the board for everyone to copy.)

Jeff's analysis of these incidents showed very clearly how the 'difference in feeling' was being generated. It had to do with how the two teachers regarded the culture of the Aboriginal children. It could not be reduced to general competencies, for both teachers handled their records, the setting and marking of work, time on task, the noise level, discipline, coverage of the curriculum, and so on, with similar expertise. And in terms of other competencies they were similarly praising and encouraging participation; as laid out in the syllabus the high absentee class teacher was even competently modelling the kind of language children are expected to use in a report. The difference lay rather in the teachers' expectations of and attitudes to the children's performance and contributions; what they valued and how they felt about them in fact.

The more experienced teacher had spent some time with Aboriginals and had a sympathetic understanding of their culture; she was more 'laid-back' and had naturally developed a 'sharing' atmosphere in which all children could participate from their own experience in their own terms. She persisted with getting Merline to tell a story because she interpreted 'Nothing' as indicating reluctance rather than literally nothing. In a subsequent interview the low absentee class teacher spoke of her belief in the importance of getting Aboriginal children to bring their culture and experiences out in the classroom. In contrast, the high absentee class teacher had a much more formal approach, partly because she felt she needed to retain more control of the class, but also because she believed that a major purpose of school was to enable Aboriginal children to assimilate and achieve in the terms of the dominant school culture. For that reason she accepted Marcia's contribution as true, but not as the way it needed to be expressed.

In some ways, then, what both of these teachers were doing was 'good practice' for which they had good reasons. But it was not an easy situation. All teachers experience difficultly balancing conflicting cultural values in class, whether they are due to differences in race or language, class or gender. The difference here lay in the teachers' view of what was good practice and the extent to which the children were expected to conform to it. One teacher tended to incorporate the Aboriginal children's experiences and values into her class because that was how those children were; the other tended to exclude them because how those children were was not how they were supposed to be in class. Thus the teachers acted differently because of who they were: they had had different experiences in life, and so interpreted similar things differently. What the children had to say meant different things to them.

Those differences in the teachers' being and value could only be revealed and explained by interpreting what they did in their classes. Once a number of such incidents had been compared and analysed, both could see and understand how the way each regarded the culture of her Aboriginal children was informing her professional judgement. It was then possible for the teachers to decide if and how they would change their views and how a changed view would change their classroom practices.

THEORY, PRACTICE AND PROFESSIONAL JUDGEMENT

In one way or another, professional judgement is always based on theory, whether it is a teacher's 'theory-in-use' or their 'espoused theory' (Argryis 1980). The basis of scientific theory is the empirical world, and the empirical world of teachers is their practice. If teachers' professional judgement is to be scientific, then one must have theories of practice. Unfortunately, in teaching, theory and practice are all too often dichotomised. This is not a single dichotomy produced just by the well-recognised conceptual barriers that exist between the realms of classroom practice and the theories that are said to inform and explain it. Theory and practice are also dichotomised by well-organised social barriers such as those between the people concerned, between school teachers and university academics. These social barriers are institutionalised in many ways, particularly in differing interests and work practices. Over the past decade I have worked on these social barriers because they appear to be more immediately tractable and amenable to change than the conceptual gaps between theory and practice, different theories, and different practices. I have tried to take on teachers' interests in the practical and to mesh our work through collaboration. The interesting and hopeful thing to have come out of this attempt is that the conceptual dichotomies appear to be produced by the social, for when one deals with the social barriers between practitioners and theoreticians, the conceptual dichotomies seem also to disappear.

The reason for this is that a conceptual theory–practice gap is frequently caused by attempts to apply theory generated elsewhere (in psychology or sociology, for instance) to teaching. When one works the other way round, when one becomes involved in theorising teachers' experiences, this gap always disappears. One cannot chant the old saw that, 'It's all very well in theory but it will not work in practice' when the theory is an attempt to explain what is working in practice. How can there be a theory–practice gap when one is constructing theory of the practice? Yet very little educational theory has yet been constructed in this way: most 'educational' theory has in fact been produced in what are often mistakenly called the 'foundation' disciplines of education. A number of problems have resulted.

An idea such as 'motivation', for instance, has tended to be dealt with in strictly psychological terms, such as a concern with an 'intrinsic/extrinsic' distinction. Unfortunately, psychological concerns on their own are inappropriate to teaching because teachers actually teach a set curriculum in a social group, which means that they are always dealing with motivation in terms of getting a group of students to do particular things (see Egan 1983). It is not much help to a teacher with a class of differently motivated students, that research on motivation has demonstrated that extrinsic rewards can lead to intrinsic motivation, but that using extrinsic rewards with intrinsically motivated students can lower their motivation. Teachers already know from experience that the difficult part is usually getting students to start and finish work, so their concerns are rather how to stimulate and maintain interest. If one were beginning with teachers' classroom experiences, then one would perhaps work on a theory of interest that includes social relations, the nature and substance of the task, and students' interests.

This suggests that what is often perceived as a gap between the application of a theory and practice is actually a gap between different theories, between the theory of researchers and the theory of teachers. This can be illustrated by the way in which educators can blame teachers for not implementing Piaget's idea of the construction of knowledge. Piaget's constructivist ideas are usually given to teachers with the idea that young children are less logical than adults; indeed, I have heard it said that because they are at Piaget's 'concrete operations' stage they cannot yet think abstractly. Teachers' experience tells them that children can think highly abstractly and are ruthless logicians, on which knowledge they have constructed their own theory of what children can do and why. The theory–practice gap in this case is a theory–theory gap.

I have tried to summarise this in Figure 4.

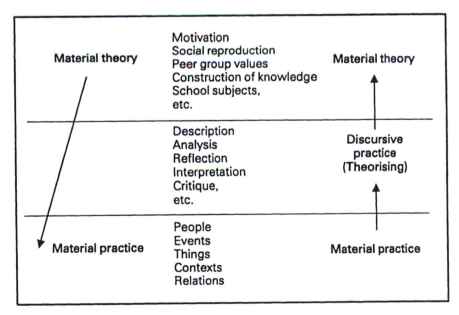

Figure 4   Theory and practice

On the left we have a representation of what tends to happen in the traditional teacher education model where teachers are taught the theories of the 'foundation' disciplines in universities. Attempts to get teachers to apply theories taken out of their context in other disciplines to their work usually fail because they do not either engage teacher's practice or develop in teachers the discursive practices necessary to translate from theory to practice. On the right is the critical incident approach which begins with material practice and creates theories through involving teachers in the processes of theorising. This is a 'grounded theory' approach (Glaser and Strauss 1967) in which incidents from teachers' practice are theorised.

The importance of all of this is that teachers suffer professionally because their professional judgements are often misjudged. In some situations their judgements are said to be misinformed because they do not use academics' 'educational' theories to form them: in others their judgements go unrecognised because what they are judging is not part of a formally articulated and researched theory. In this situation teachers are effectively denied the expertise of academics in improving their judgements. One way to improve this state of affairs is through the construction, documentation and theorisation of critical incidents. The approach enables teachers and academics to work collaboratively on teachers' experiences rendered material as accounts of classroom incidents.

A COLLABORATIVE APPROACH TO CRITICAL INCIDENTS

There are many different forms of collaboration, so it is important to lay out what I consider to be the basis of the working agreement between an academic and a teacher. At the time of writing the agreement involves the following:

1   A shared commitment to the necessity for the research;
2   A research agenda consisting of topics of mutual concern;
3   Equally shared control over the research processes;
4   Outcomes that are of equal value to all participants in professional terms;
5   Using 'fairness' to inform matters of justice amongst participants.

The model I am currently using for working on critical incidents with teachers involves the use of teacher-written incidents which I regard as essential to set the research agenda and ensure that the teachers are the principal audience for the research. It is a method derived from an action research approach that is common to most kinds of reflective teaching, with a slightly different cycle for analysis and theorisation. The first cycle is principally for the teacher and the other principally for the researcher. The moment of analysis in which the two cycles overlap, is where the majority of collaboration takes place.

Considering the two cycles separately first, the teacher's cycle is the traditional action research cycle as suggested by Lewin (1946). It consists of initial observation of current practice, analysis of the observational data, planning changed practice, implementation, observation of the new practice... etc. It is that over which the teacher, being the practitioner, has to have control. On the other hand, the re-

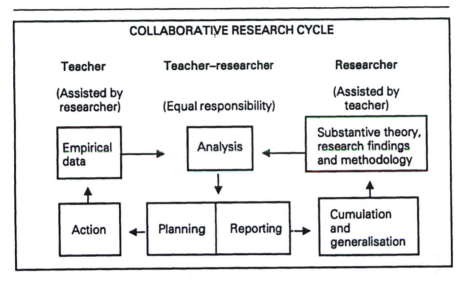

COLLABORATIVE RESEARCH CYCLE

Teacher	Teacher–researcher	Researcher
(Assisted by researcher)	(Equal responsibility)	(Assisted by teacher)

Figure 5   A model for collaborative action research

searcher's cycle consists of using analytic procedures and knowledge of theory in the interpretation of the data, documentation of the whole teachers' cycle, and then cumulation and verification towards the development of grounded theory.

In this approach, collaboration in terms of equality of input is probably at its strongest in the moment of analysis. Although collaboration means that the value for both parties should be mutual and symmetrical, it does not mean that they have to contribute in the same way, or gain the same outcome. Indeed, it is the very differences between contributions and expectations that make collaboration so strong methodologically. It allows for either researcher or teacher to generate an analysis, and the other party to critique and verify it. Thus whilst the researcher draws upon their specialist knowledge of existing theories and analytics for one explanation of the data, the teacher draws upon other relevant experience and their critical judgement in a process of case-to-case generalisation to produce another kind of analysis. This can be shown in a third variation of Figure 4 (see Figure 6).

The difference here is that there is now a two-way interaction between existing theories and teachers' practice as what the academic already knows is brought to bear upon the teaching incidents. This process has been present in most of the critical incident analyses in this book (e.g. correspondence theory in Incident 7: *Finishing work*), but an extended example, where I used theories of communicative competence to explain an incident, is to be found in Tripp 1987).

The other phases of the model are more co-operative than collaborative: one or other party has to have the final say because they must take responsibility for the consequences. In the planning moment, for instance, the teacher must have the authority to decide what to do, because it is they who have to enact the plan in their classroom. Ideally, they should be able to generate the plan together, but ultimately the researcher is but the teacher's critical friend: they can only make suggestions, offer advice and alternatives, and act as a sounding board for ideas. In the observation moment, however, the researcher can act as a second or outside observer for the teacher.

The professional critical incident research file is crucial to the data moment in this model, and both teacher and researcher have equally important but different roles to play in it. Critical incident research files are a good way of enabling the practitioners to set the collaborative research agenda because, though it is the teachers' choice of what items to record in their critical incident research files, experienced critical friends and trained researchers are also necessary in this process if the teacher is to avoid the effects of minimisation, denial and delusion which threaten all forms of self-reflection (Mellody 1989: 129–33). So it is in the data and analysis moments that collaboration is most clearly realised: far from excluding teachers from the choice of the research question and casting them as the research object of an outside 'professional' researcher, teachers make their own choices and are active, self-reflective researchers into their own practice and situation.

For the researcher, the teacher's interpretation of the data and experiences as the teacher's critical friend provide the data that they then use in their research. But what they do with that data, the conclusions they draw from it and the theories they build, are similarly open to the critique of the teacher. Thus the teacher might draw

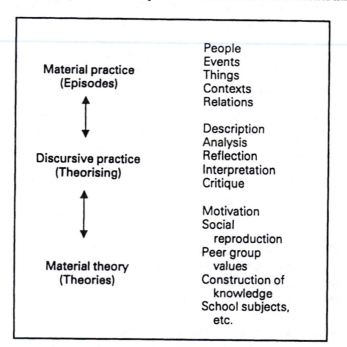

Figure 6   Theory–practice process with teacher-researcher in collaboration

the researcher's attention to further or counter-instances of a particular phenomenon which the researcher must either incorporate into a theoretical framework which is broader than the original data, or treat the instances differently. In this way the learning is symmetrical (the teacher learns as much as the researcher), but the substantive outcomes are quite different: the teacher's gains are principally in the form of improved practices and understanding of their own teaching, whilst the researcher gains data for theorising schooling and teacher's practical knowledge. It is in terms of those outcomes and the processes by which they are achieved that this form of research is collaborative.[1]

To summarise the approach, I believe the collaborative model is one where teachers can make their own choices and are active researchers and self-reflective interpreters of their own practice and situation. For the outside researcher, working collaboratively means that the teacher's experiences in those roles are the research data, so the overall substantive outcomes are markedly different: the teacher's gains are principally in the form of improved practices and understanding of their teaching, whilst the researcher gains data for theorising schooling and teacher's practical knowledge. It is in terms of those outcomes and the processes by which they are achieved that the nature of the research must be determined. Collaborative research in the classroom thus takes place between two consenting but somewhat schizophrenic professionals who share a common bond: a teacher-researcher and a researcher-teacher educator.

THE TASK AHEAD

The main task suggested by this book is to enable teachers to develop the scope of and their expertise in professional judgement. The critical incident approach leading from practice through diagnosis and reflection to critical interpretation is but one way in which this could be done. And as an advocate of the kind of diagnostic teaching produced by the examination of critical incidents, I am necessarily involved in the attempt to develop the approach by improving the methods, producing more and better quality examples, telling others about it, and so on. But behind these efforts lies an agenda for why one should use a diagnostic method rather than any other, such as reflective teaching.

One compelling reason for using critical incidents is that the conditions under which teachers work and are educated and certified are rapidly changing. What many teacher-educators see as two major threats to the quality of their work have recently appeared. One is the general move towards specifying professional teaching behaviour in terms of the competencies required; and the other is the particularly British and Australian move to remove teacher education students from tertiary institutions, requiring them to spend up to 80 per cent of their preparation time working in schools. Under present structures this is likely to lead to a cycle of reproduction in which purely practical competencies would dominate, further deprofessionalising teaching. But using critical incidents in some of the ways advocated here could actually turn both of these moves to advantage. The minimum practical competencies necessary to professional teaching may perhaps best be learned from expert practitioners in the reality of the job situation. But as merely practical competencies are insufficient for professional practice, the creation and analysis of critical incidents is a good way to develop the equally necessary skills of informed professional judgement.

In the longer term a more important reason for teacher and academic collaboration in critical incidents has to do with the nature and politics of knowledge in education, whose and what kind of purposes that knowledge best serves. As I wrote right at the start of this book, it was only when I recognised the fact that I had been very successful in the classroom when I was very ignorant of what academics considered knowledge essential to teaching, that I became aware of the difference between the knowledge of academics and the knowledge of teachers. It has since become clear that most academic educational knowledge is of very little use to teachers and that teachers' knowledge and understanding of their practice is seriously under-represented and discounted in the university discipline of education. This difference has created and maintained deep the divisions between teachers and academics and so between practice and theory which I believe are primarily responsible for the under-valuing of school teaching. I see critical incidents as a particularly effective way of redressing these imbalances.

In contrast to the dominant form of academic educational knowledge, the knowledge gained from critical incidents is deeply contextualised in the culture of classrooms and the actions and values of teachers. Not only is it both immediate and real for teachers, but it explains teaching from their point of view. Thus the interpretation of critical incidents offers a way to involve teachers as both clients and partners in research on the understanding and improvement of their practice. It appears to me that the most promising means of improving teaching is by grounding educational research (and thus theory) in the realities of teachers' everyday experience. Overall, I believe that an approach based on the interpretation of critical incidents has the potential to change the nature of the teaching profession by dealing with the fundamental practical, political and epistemological problems of education in teachers' terms.

Notes

AFTERTHOUGHT

1 Following common colloquial usage, I use 'their' and 'they' as ungendered singular and plural pronouns throughout this book.

INTRODUCTION

1 For a more detailed treatment of this issue, see Tripp 1990a.
2 The use of critical incidents as a means of raising issues for collaborative classroom action and other kinds of research will be the subject of a companion volume expected to be completed in 1993.

1 PROBLEMATIC AND PRACTICE

1 My thanks to my colleague, Bob Hodge for pointing out that the difficulty here is that 'problematic' is a transliteration of the French noun *la problématique* which sounds like an English adjective ('symptomatic', 'emphatic', etc.).
2 As Althusser and Balibar (1977) put it: [science] '...can only pose problems on the terrain and within the horizon of a definite theoretical structure, its problematic, which constitutes its absolute and definite condition of possibility, and hence the absolute determination of the forms in which all problems must be posed, at any given moment in the science.'
3 This conclusion is not excepted, for a reading of Althusser and Balibar reveals that the analysis of problematic has its own problematic, which informs the kind of information one has to collect, and the kind of analysis that is necessary in order to perceive problematics.
4 Note that I am registering the presence of this problematic, not judging it. On certain grounds one can argue that a message about gender differences is appropriate. The same division is made in most sports for the same reason. The real danger is that it can become over-generalised so that girls come to believe that they cannot compete with boys – period. This works to the disadvantage of girls when, for instance, girls and boys perceive maths and science to be 'boys' subjects'. But to teach students to recognise discrimination and to judge whether it is just or not, can be useful.
5 He knew both his and her view of the situation; she knew only hers. Whilst knowledge is power, not knowing is one of the more devious hallmarks of power. If the powerful do not know that the powerless has another, different view of the matter, then they do

not need to defend their view or take the other view into account. So they can act according to their view alone, and thus oppress the powerless without recognising the oppression.

For instance, supposing that the teacher in this example assumes that the boy also thinks the problem is his laziness because she does not know (because she ensures that he is not able to tell her) that he is actually bored by the work she sets, she can continue to consider her lessons fine and treat him as if he were plain lazy, without ever having to prove him or her lessons anything other.

6   Again, thanks to Bob Hodge for pointing out that there was a similar asymmetry between myself and this teacher as there was between herself and John. In much the same way that she had judged John to be lazy, I had judged her to be unobservant and unreflective; and in much the same way that John was telling her something about himself and the work she set him by not completing it, she was doing the same with my requirement that she write a critical incident. Furthermore, in writing about John she was presenting me with a similar case for consideration.

7   Indeed, once teachers have experienced the collaborative problematisation of their practice, they are able to help us problematise ours. For example, a teacher asked me if I had ever paid any attention to how I made my accounts of my critical incidents anonymous: by always using names such as John, Dick, Mary and Jane, I was not only unfairly stigmatising the people who really had those names, but (because they are all so common) also increasing the likelihood of people's thinking I was using their experiences directly.

2   INTERPRETATION: CREATING CRITICAL INCIDENTS

1   See, for instance, the work of M. Hammersley and A. Hargreaves (1983) or S. Ball (1987).
2   My thanks here to my colleague, Sue Willis, who introduced me to this broader notion of diagnostic teaching.
3   This is one reason for the failure of the many attempts to reduce effective teaching to a set of technical knowledge and routines. If the teacher is successful with one approach to discipline, students can always produce behaviours that required some other approach.
4   I am aware that in other fields (such as literature) one does not have to choose a single meaning, but can accept several different, even contradictory, meanings. More often then not in teaching, however, one does have to give preference to a single meaning because one has to act on it. One usually has to decide whether behaviour is bad or not, whether work is acceptable or not, and so on. It is that imperative that creates the dilemmas of teaching.
5   See for a good example Lyons' (1973) comparison of English–French 'The cat sat on the mat'.
6   Historically, modern Western medical practice is an exception in terms of the limits of its diagnostic procedures: most cultures do not accept an identified disease as the primary cause of an illness; they also require an explanation of what caused the disease itself to occur in the first place. Only recently has Western medicine begun to look for the causes of the causes of diseases rather than merely to describe the action of the disease itself. A simple illustration is the way in which traditional African tribespeople believe that illness is always caused by someone's witchcraft. Today this does not mean that they need to deny that bacteria are causing an infection, but that they also want to know who caused the bacteria to grow in that particular child at that time and why they did so. Knowledge of bacteria is not therefore necessarily at odds with a belief in witchcraft, any more than a knowledge of evolution has caused Christians to deny God any role in creation: in both cases, the diagnosis merely accounts for how it was done by whoever it was who is believed to have done it. Diagnosis of the cause of a diagnosed disease is much less certain than diagnosis of the disease itself.

7 Note that I reflected on an episode; I did not create a critical incident from it at this point. To do so I would only have to have asked questions such as, 'Why else might this be happening?' and 'What does the reason it happens tell me about these students, this subject, the text, my course?'

3 FOUR APPROACHES TO THE ANALYSIS OF INCIDENTS

1 A 'non-event' analysis would raise the diagnostic alternative: discovering why the child is throwing her food away, and changing that.

5 THE CRITICAL INCIDENT FILE: STRUCTURE AND PURPOSES

1 When part of an action research project, critical incident files are essentially public records: they constitute the 'evidence' about what happened, an account of events and ideas that have shaped the teacher-researcher's perceptions and actions. The requirements for public evidence are quite different from those of personal record: the public must be told what the writer (but not the public) already knows. I do not include that aspect of preparing critical incidents or files for publication as a part of the file process itself, because it is a further process, one that can sometimes be done by someone other than the original author.

2 It can, as always, however, be re-considered and extended. It raises more general questions such as, 'Should we take "external" factors such as the weather more into consideration in our planning? If so then how?' 'Ditto, with "internal" factors such as how I'm feeling'.

3 I have discussed this point in more detail in Tripp 1985 and 1991b.

4 For more detailed discussion on these processes, see Tripp 1990a and 1993.

6 AN EXAMPLE OF A CRITICAL INCIDENT FILE

1 'Sharing chairs' usually means two people have but one chair between them. Ben had to abandon this normal meaning of the phrase for a specialist mathematical one in which, when chairs were shared between people, each person had two each.

7 AUTOBIOGRAPHICAL INCIDENTS AND CLASSROOM PRACTICE

1 That is not to say that to look at the past in this way means that we thereby allow it to determine the future, just the opposite in fact. One way to break with the past is to identify practices that have become habits and examine them, revealing what has to be changed to achieve different outcomes. It is also important to remember that it is sometimes more freeing to think first about what it is we would like to achieve regardless of our past or present practice, before using historical understanding to recognise what we must do to achieve it.

2 This is actually a good example of the way in which a memory can surface when appropriately stimulated and given adequate time. Several months after writing this draft, I was reading another piece when I suddenly recalled a particular teacher I did not like. I began exploring what I could remember about him, and decided that I had not liked him because he was unpredictable and unfair. Searching for an example, I suddenly and very vividly remembered my first clash with him, probably in about the third lesson. Something someone said had begun a chain of thought, which I was following instead of what was happening in the class. He suddenly sprang a question on me, and as I had not been

listening I could not answer it. I had apparently been staring out of the window, so he gave me a four page essay on 'Windows'. After the lesson I tried to explain what had happened and to tell him what I had been thinking about, but was simply told not to make excuses. I said I was not making excuses, and got a 6-page essay for my pains. Now, having recalled the experience, I can still remember how angry I felt at the time. As also often happens, one powerful incident contains more than one message: I have since used that same incident to illustrate how the powerful are able to define the world in their own interests: defining my 'reason' as an 'excuse' legitimated the unfair punishment.

3   With reference to the opening comment (that the past should be used to change the present rather than allowing it to determine it) this is also a good example of using the present to determine the past: the act of reclassifying the significance of the incident changed its nature. See also Tripp (1993b).

4   As I have pointed out elsewhere (Tripp 1993), this is not unproblematic; there is still a real danger of the biographical process, as it is now frequently being performed, of becoming yet another form of 'studying down' (Bell 1978), so that it is of greater value to the academics who build their reputations by performing the research, than to the teachers who so willingly collaborate with them.

8 SOCIALLY CRITICAL ACTION AND ANALYSIS

1   Parts of this chapter were delivered as an invited contribution to the opening keynote symposium of the annual conference of the West Australian Institute of Educational Research, 30 August 1991.

2   It is important to note that this work is not without criticism from others working according to the principles of critical theory, especially from feminist perspectives (see for instance, Ellsworth (1989) and Lather (1991).

3   I find the most useful books here to be Carr and Kemmis (1983), Kemmis, Cole and Suggett (1983) and Grundy (1987).

4   'Critical pedagogy' is the term usually used to refer to what happens when someone teaches according to principles of social justice; and 'critical action research' refers to a process in which one plans and evaluates one's teaching according to an understanding of the social justice of the situation gained from researching it.

5   I think it important not to ignore the distinction between the emancipatory interest and a socially critical approach. At its simplest, emancipation is freedom from existing constraints, and what makes it possible is the development of a socially critical consciousness. Given that teachers' primary concern is with improving their practice, the technical, reflective and critical do not just offer different ways of regarding and acting in a situation, but are ways of thinking and being. Further, the emancipatory interest is always collective, whereas all critiques can be individual.

6   This is because the children can still intend to learn through wishing to follow the instructions till they learn what it is they will have learned by following the instructions.

7   For the purposes of this paper I am not problematising the content of the lesson itself. Were I working with this teacher on re-planning an actual lesson I would suggest that the term 'prediction' be dropped altogether, and the lesson should perhaps begin with a demonstration of the fact that both estimation and measurement involve approximation. One could then move on to the facts that the accuracy (and therefore the unit) required of a measurement depends upon the measurer's purpose, and that the accuracy of measurement and estimation can be improved with practice.

8   I refuse to make the common contrast between 'school' and 'real life', because it is a means by which certain interest groups devalue school learning by implying that it is 'unreal', that is, 'pretend' and 'play'. School is but one of a number of spheres of life, all

of which are equally 'real'. It is difficult to find a satisfactory alternative, but until a better one is found, I shall refer to 'school life' and 'other spheres of life'.

9   CRITICAL INCIDENTS AND PROFESSIONAL JUDGEMENT

1   My thanks here to my colleague, Dr Annette Patterson, for pointing out the need to qualify the bald question, and to Marguerite Laurence for offering the following alternative reading:

> Subconsciously, Troy is not going to be fooled, because a double message has been delivered. At best he will be puzzled by his own continuing confusion. The problem is that the whole class (which is made up of similarly individual people) is made to feel their reaction is inappropriate, which doesn't benefit Troy but does save the teacher's face. I think it was a very slick piece of sleight of hand, but although some damage may have been mitigated, another kind may well have resulted.

Clearly both analyses have their own validity, but it is not necessary to choose which one is 'correct'; one can accept the contradictory views as explaining different aspects of the same episode; the only choice necessary to professional judgement is how to develop the most beneficial aspects and diminish the least. Such are the dilemmas of teaching.

2   A major exception to this is the work of Eisner (1979) though even this has come in for some sharp criticism from researchers with a strong rationalist bent (cf Smith 1984).

3   I cannot be certain that she was not able to explain her diagnosis, but suggest that this is the case on the grounds that she did not comment on the incident when she went over the lesson in detail with the observer.

4   One might note that this is a practice-based form of theorising very different from the way a traditional philosopher of education would have dealt with the matter of discipline, perhaps through an analysis of the concept. It is not that the analysis is not 'philosophical', but that in it the teacher stands quite differently in relation to the subject matter of what is usually taught as the philosophy of education. It is that which has profound implications for the development of knowledge in education, and the practice of education as a discipline.

5   I stress 'my' because such analyses are always provisional and revisable, and they need to be negotiated and shared with the other participants before any claims of objectivity or validity are made. My analysis is offered as an example of the kind of points that should emerge from the incident as an agenda for reflection and further investigation, not to 'prove' anything in an 'objective' fashion. As Glaser and Strauss (1967) point out, hypotheses do not have to be true to be useful.

6   I hope that those who believe teaching is best learned by apprenticeship will pause to think about this incident.

CONCLUSION

1   My thanks to my colleague Alison Lee for pointing out that in social terms the outcomes are still far from symmetrical. The teacher may improve their classroom practice, but the researcher gains kudos and public recognition in the much higher status world of academe. Clearly this is true for me: I enjoy a far wider recognition of my work in this book than do my collaborating teachers who are necessarily anonymous here. It is a serious problem, but one which would be greatly mitigated if this work led to better public recognition of the importance and value of teachers' work.

Select bibliography

Althusser, L. and Balibar, E. (1977) *Reading Capital*, Paris: New Left Books.
Apple, M. (1982) *Education and Power*, London: Routledge and Kegan Paul.
—— (1986) *Teachers and Texts*, London: Routledge and Kegan Paul.
Argryis, C. (1980) *Inner Contradictions of Rigorous Research*, New York: Academic Press.
Aronowitz, S. and Giroux, H. (1985) *Education under Siege: the Conservative, Liberal and Radical Debate over Schooling*, South Hadley, Mass.: Bergin & Garvey.
Ball, S. (1987) *The Micro-politics of the School*, London: Methuen.
Barnes, D. (1969) 'Language in the secondary classroom', in D. Barnes, J. Britton and H. Rosen (eds) *Language, the Learner and the School*, Harmondsworth: Penguin.
—— (1975) *From Communication to Curriculum*, Harmondsworth: Penguin.
Barthes, R. (1973) *Mythologies*, London: Paladin.
Bateson, G. (1973) *Steps towards an Ecology of Mind*, New York: Paladin.
Bell, C. (1978) 'Studying the locally powerful', in C. Bell and S. Encel (eds) *Inside the Whale*, Sydney: Pergamon.
Berger, P. J. and Luckman, T. (1966) *The Social Construction of Reality*, Harmondsworth: Penguin.
Berlak, A. and Berlak, H. (1981) *Dilemmas of Schooling*, London: Methuen.
Boomer, G. (ed.) (1982) *Negotiating the Curriculum*, Sydney: Ashton.
Britton, J. (1969) 'Talking to learn;, in D. Barnes, J. Britton and H. Rosen (eds) *Language, the Learner and the School*, Harmondsworth: Penguin.
—— (1972) *Language and Learning*, Harmondsworth: Penguin.
Bruner, J. S. (1971) *Toward a Theory of Instruction*, Cambridge, Mass.: Harvard University Press.
Carr, W. and Kemmis, S. (1983) *Becoming Critical: Knowing through Action Research*, Geelong (Australia): Deakin University Press; also available from Falmer Press.
de Bono, E. (1987) *The CoRT Thinking Course*, London: Pergamon.
Delamont, S. (1976) 'Beyond Flanders' Fields: The relationship of subject-matter and individuality to classroom style', in M. Stubbs and S. Delamont (eds) *Explorations in Classroom Observation*, Chichester: J. Wiley & Sons.
Dunkin, M. J. and Biddle, B. J. (1974) *The Study of Teaching*, New York: Holt Rinehart & Winston.
Egan, K. (1983) *Education and Psychology*, London: Methuen.
Eisner, E. W. (1979) *The Educational Imagination*, New York: Macmillan.
Elliott, J. and Adleman, C. (1976) *The Ford Teaching Project*, Cambridge: Cambridge Institute of Education.
Ellsworth, E. (1989) 'Why doesn't this feel empowering? Working through the repressive myths of critical pedagogy', *Harvard Education Review* 59(3): 297–324.

Flynn, J. M. (1972) 'Evaluation and the fate of innovations', *Educational Technology*, April: 52–4.

Freire, P. (1972) *Pedagogy of the Oppressed*, Harmondsworth: Penguin.

Frow, J. (1983) 'Reading as system and as practice', *Comparative Criticism Yearbook 5*, Cambridge: Cambridge University Press.

Giroux, H. (1983) *Theory and Resistence in Education: A Pedagogy for the Opposition*, London: Heinemann.

Glaser, B. G. and Strauss, A. L. (1967) *The Discovery of Grounded Theory: Strategies for Qualitative Research*, Chicago: Aldine.

Green, W. (1985) 'WA Ministry of Education English Syllabus Development Document 1: English Syllabus Outline Discussion Paper', mimeo from the author, now at Deakin University School of Education, Waurn Ponds, Geelong, Victoria.

Green, W. and Reid, J. (1986) 'English teaching, in-service and action research: the Kewdale project', *English in Australia* 75: 4–21.

Grundy, S. J. (1982) 'Three modes of action research', *Curriculum Perspectives*, 2(3): 23–34.

—— (1987) *Curriculum: Product or Praxis?*, Lewes: Falmer Press.

Habermas, J. (1972) *Knowledge and Human Interest*, London: Heinemann.

Hall, S. (1989) Fieldwork observation from 'A teacher's use of her tacit teaching knowledge in the self-evaluation of her professional practice', unpubd PhD research, Murdoch University, Western Australia.

Hammersley, M. and Hargreaves, A. (1983) *Curriculum Practice: Some Sociological Case Studies*, Lewes: Falmer Press.

Hodge, R. I. and Tripp, D. H. (1986) *Children and Television: A Semiotic Approach*, Stanford: Policity/Stanford University Press.

Homberger, E. and Charmley, J. (1988) *The Troubled Face of Biography*, London: Macmillan.

Hudson, L. (1972) *The Cult of the Fact*, London: Cape.

Ingvarson, L. (1986) 'With critical friends, who needs enemies?' in P. Fensham, C. Power, D. Tripp and S. Kemmis, *Alienation from Schooling*, London: Routledge & Kegan Paul.

Johnson, D. W. and Johnson, R. T. (1975) *Learning Together and Alone*, Englewood Cliffs, NJ: Prentice Hall.

Kemmis, S., Cole, P. and Suggett, D. (1983) *Towards the Socially Critical School*, Melbourne: Victorian Institute of Secondary Education.

Lather, P. (1991) *Getting Smart: Feminist Research and Pedagogy within the Post-modern*, London: Routledge.

Lewin, K. (1946) 'Action research and minority problems', *Journal of Social Issues* 2: 34–6.

Lister, D. P. and Zeichner, K. M. (1987) 'Reflective teacher education and moral deliberation', *Journal of Teacher Education* 38(6): 2–8.

Livingstone, D. W. (1987) *Critical Pedagogy and Cultural Power*, South Hadley, Mass.: Bergin & Garvey.

Lyons, J. (1973) 'Structuralism and linguistics', in D. Robey (ed.) *Structuralism: An Introduction*, Oxford: Oxford University Press.

Lyons, N. (1990) 'Dilemmas of knowing: Ethical and epistemological dimensions of teachers' work and development', *Harvard Educational Review* 60(2): 159–80.

Mellody, P. (1989) *Facing Codependence*, San Francisco: Harper & Row.

Mezirow, J. (1981) 'A critical theory of adult learning and education', *Adult Education*, 32: 3–24.

Mills, C. Wright (1959) *The Sociological Imagination*, Harmondsworth: Penuin.

Open University (1973) Course E341 Methods of Educational Enquiry (Block 3: Data Collection) Milton Keynes: The Open University.

Pinar, W. (1986) 'Autobiography and Architecture of Self', paper presented at AERA, San Francisco, April.

Polanyi, M. and Prosch, H. (1975) *Personal Knowledge in Meaning*, London: University of Chicago Press.

Popkewitz, T. S. (1984) *Paradigm and Ideology in Educational Research*, Lewes: Falmer Press.

Pratte, R. (1986) 'Educational policy and teacher educators', *Australian Journal of Teacher Education* 11(2): 9–18.

Schön, D. (1983) *The Reflective Practitioner: How Professionals Think in Action*, New York: Basic Books.

Shulman, L. S. (1987) 'Knowledge and teaching: foundations of the new reform', *Harvard Educational Review* 57(1): 1–22.

Smith, R. (1984) *The New Aesthetic Curriculum Theorists and their Astonishing Ideas*, Vancouver: Centre for the Study of Curriculum and Instruction, University of British Columbia.

Smyth, W. J. (1985) 'Developing a critical practice of clinical supervision', *Journal of Curriculum Studies* 17(1): 1–15.

Stenhouse, L. (1975) *An Introduction to Curriculum Research and Development*, London: Heinemann Educational.

Tom, A. (1984) *Teaching as a Moral Craft*, New York: Longman.

Tripp, D. H. (1983) 'Co-authorship and negotiation: the interview as act of creation', *Interchange* 14(3): 32–45.

—— (1984a) 'Cinderella curriculum and the sibling disciplines', paper presented at the annual conference of the Australian Association for Research in Education, Perth, Nov. 1984.

—— (1984b) 'From autopilot to critical consciousness: problematizing successful teaching', paper presented at the Sixth Conference on Curriculum Theory and Pracice, Bergamo, Dayton, Ohio.

—— (1986) 'Greenfield: Schooling, alienation and employment', in P. Fensham, C. Power, D. Tripp and S. Kemmis *Alienation from Schooling*, London: Routledge & Kegan Paul.

—— (1987) 'Teachers, journals and collaborative research', in J. Smyth (ed.) *Educating Teachers: Changing the Nature of Professional Knowledge*, Lewes: Falmer Press.

—— (1989) 'The idea of meta-curriculum as a common national curriculum', *Curriculum Perspectives* 9(4): 79–88.

—— (1990a) 'The ideology of educational research', *Discourse: The Australian Journal of Educational Studies* 10(2): 51–74.

—— (1990b) 'Socially critical action research', *Theory Into Practice* 24(3): 158–66.

—— (1991a) *Doing a Humpty on Curriculum: Suggestions for Avoiding a Definition*, mimeo from the author at Murdoch University, Western Australia, 6150, 4.

—— (1991b) *Theorising Teaching*, Introduction to Murdoch University course, E562: Theory and Practice in Education.

—— (1993a) 'On the role and characteristics of collaborative research in education', in P. P. Grimmett and M. L. Wodlinger (eds) *Collaborative Research in Teacher Education*, Toronto: Kagan and Woo.

—— (1993b) 'On Pedagogoautobiographicopraxicomethodology: teachers' lives and critical incidents', *Qualitative Studies in Education* 7: footnote.

Walker, R. (1980) 'Making sense and losing meaning', in H. Simons (ed.) *Toward a Science of the Singular*. CARE occasional publication no. 10, Norwich, Centre for Applied Research in Education, University of East Anglia.

Woods, P. (1992) 'Critical events in education', paper given at British Educational Research Association 18th Annual Conference, University of Stirling, Aug. 26–9.

—— *Critical Incidents in Teaching and Learning*, Lewes: Falmer Press.

Young, M. F. D. (1971) *Knowledge and Control*, London: Collier Macmillan.

Index

Printed in the United States
112229LV00001B/16/A